AF255114

Unearthing the past
... a dubious family history

Copyright © 2024

All Rights Reserved

ISBN 978-0-6455853-9-1 Paperback

ISBN 978-1-7637654-0-5 E-book

Published by: IngramSpark Australia (2024)

Acknowledgments

Thanks very much to my friend Anna Rosner Blay and my husband Peter Levy for taking time to proof read and put in their two-bob's worth.

Unearthing the past

... a dubious family history

Sharon Hurst

Contents

Preface

1 The past emerges ____ 1

2 1966 – The year of the crush ______________________________ 4

3 London 1935 – Harry practises all manner of things _________ 7

4 Time to settle down ______________________________________ 10

5 July 1939 – The Big Apple ________________________________ 16

6 1939 – The world at war __________________________________ 21

7 1970 – First love ____ 28

8 1976 – Decision crisis ____________________________________ 35

9 There is life out there ____________________________________ 37

10 1924–41 – Amazing Grace _______________________________ 40

11 1941 – Grace goes to war ________________________________ 45

12 1943 – Harry can't take it any more _______________________ 49

13 Grace chases her dream _________________________________ 55

14 1946 – Harry heads to Palestine __________________________ 57

15 July 1947 – Harry on the high seas ________________________ 60

16 Life on the wicked stage _________________________________ 64

17 Harry overplays his hand ________________________________ 67

18 Theatrical shenanigans __________________________________ 71

19 When Angela met Harry _________________________________ 77

20 A childhood memory – those old letters ____________________ 80

21 Secrets of the childhood trunk ____________________________ 82

22 RIP Harry ____ 85

23 The fateful letters re-emerge _____________________________ 88

24 Angela and Harry start afresh Down Under _________________ 95

25 Family life becomes more fraught _________________________ 102

26 When Sarah met David __________________________________ 108

27 Life between marriages: several sad and sorry affairs __ 112

28 Are we still right together? ______________________________ 123

29 Harry misbehaves yet again ______________________________ 125

30 Angela takes an extreme step ____________________________ 127

31 Sarah revisits more men from the past _____________________ 132

32 When Harry met Helen __________________________________ 135

33 A wake-up call ____ 138

Unearthing the past
... a dubious family history

Preface

Faction (fact + fiction): Typically pejorative, it refers to a form of narrative based on real events but employing dramatic licence.

After our parents die, many of us say the same thing. "I wish I could have asked Mum or Dad about …"

Of course, after they're gone, there is so much about our parents we will never know. Even if they have told us many things about their lives, there will always be questions left to ask once it is too late. Sometimes we are lucky enough to have acquired memorabilia that provides evidence of their lives, even their deepest thoughts and secrets.

This little reflection, loosely inspired by the lives of my parents, owes some of the more truthful sections to the many letters, newspaper clippings, photographs and other random bits and pieces I inherited from them after their deaths. Some of it is reconstructed from my childhood and subsequent memories of it. Some of it takes gross liberties with the facts and imagines who could have said or done what to whom. They are not around to dispute me.

How parents affect the lives of their children, and the choices those offspring make, is the subject of many psychological studies. Witnessing a dysfunctional marriage may influence children in making similarly unsuitable choices. Sarah's experiences may or may not be reflective of my own life, but naturally the names have been changed to protect the guilty!

Chapter 1
The past emerges

Who would have thought it? Just as Sarah finally hoped she was settling into a tolerable "old age", along came something totally out of left field to upset the applecart – a pandemic, of all things! A virus that struck at random and which, at the time, had no treatment or vaccine.

How to fill the days now that everyone was in a state of semi-lockdown? No chance to hold a dinner party, visit friends or do anything that took her out of the house, other than go for a permitted brisk walk around the block. Daily exercise was still allowed, along with three other designated reasons to leave the house – shopping, medical reasons and caring for dependents.

To make matters worse, she would have to tough this one out on her own, as her husband David was overseas on business and was now essentially stranded due to all international flights being cancelled.

Perhaps it was a prime opportunity to get into some of those boxes that had been carted around each time she'd moved house over very many years. Those yellowing, peeling boxes, stuffed to the gills with papers – a testament to her life of jottings, record-taking, list-making and diarising. Not to mention hoarding of precious letters, cards and photographs. All testament to lives well – or not so well – lived. Probably most should be thrown out; but just to be sure…

Climbing up on a chair, Sarah tentatively extracted an old cardboard fruit box from the top shelf of the closet in the spare room. Careful, she told herself, don't fall now. You know you're not supposed to be climbing up on things at your age. You might have "a fall". Funny, she thought, how younger people fell over but people of her age "had a fall".

What exactly was "her age"? Sure, it was a chronological figure, but the big joke that life perpetrated on everyone who lived so long, was the ghastly fact that, inside, one still felt young, while the body betrayed the true facts of the number of years spent upon the planet.

Grappling the box down and dumping its contents unceremoniously on the bed, she began to riffle through what looked like scribbled papers and a collection of various diaries. Randomly grabbing a green-covered dog-eared diary, she opened it and carefully smoothed the bent corner of the first page. She was amazed to see how neat her writing had been back then. Now, after years of constant computer use, her handwriting was a near-illegible scrawl.

A photo was tucked between the first two pages. Strange that she hadn't filed it with her other school memorabilia. Everything about her photo collection was so ordered; how this one has escaped was anyone's guess. How young she looked in that old scratched black and white print. Perhaps aged thirteen, a short, large-breasted girl, not fat, but certainly not wafer thin. Beside her stood a scrawny young boy, baby-faced, with an impish smile. Unbeknown to her at the time, he was holding two fingers up in a V behind her head. He obviously didn't have the same crush on her that she had on him.

What was his name now? Something a bit foreign – certainly unusual for such a suburban mainstream WASPish school … Ah yes, Siggy Bjorksen. This weedy un-singular looking lad was evidence of her first crush on what she termed "a boy". All the others she'd fancied earlier on in her young life had definitely been men, so ludicrously old they could have been her father.

Ah, her father, but there was a reminiscence for another day. For now, the photo and the diary had captured her attention. They were a portal back to those high school years, the days of hopes, fears, aspirations and teenage crushes.

Chapter 2
1966 – The year of the crush

The teasing had become almost too much to bear.

The boys taunted from the desk behind, "Sarah's teacher's pet – she's a smarty-pants – she's a brain – she'll never get a boyfriend."

At least I'll get somewhere in life, she thought, not like you stupid boys who just want to disrupt the class.

She turned her attention to Mr Robb, the teacher holding court at the front of the class. Tall, with tousled black hair, slightly more casually dressed than most of the other teachers. He ran the school folk-singing group which Sarah aspired to join one of these days. For the time being he was the object of her, and most of the other girls', fantasies and giggling crushes. He'd scrawled a simultaneous equation on the board, had given the class two minutes to solve it, and was now looking expectantly at the students, many of whom had blank looks on their faces.

"So who can tell me the value of x and y in this equation?" he queried.

Sarah's hand shot up. "x is 4 and y is 6," she smugly reported, ignoring the sneers and taunts from the boys behind.

"Well done," said Mr Robb, and in that moment she felt any amount of rejection from her silly peers was worth the approval of this handsome man who smiled broadly at her, making her feel simultaneously proud, uneasy and disturbed in a way she couldn't quite put her finger on.

Sarah's home was within easy walking distance of school. Mostly she walked to school with the girl next door, who was doing her final year and probably felt it was beneath her to be seen in the company of a younger person. It made Sarah feel a bit special, a bit grown up, to be with someone so mature, especially since Elizabeth was also head prefect that year.

But most afternoons she headed home alone.

Today, basking in the glow of Mr Robb's praise, she decided to spend a little of her meagre pocket money on a small honeycomb bar and a few of her favourite sweets, mint leaves.

Entering her local milk bar, she felt her heart rise to her throat, as there he was, Siggy, standing at the counter, also ready to spend some money.

"Ten cents of humbugs," said Siggy, casting a glance in Sarah's direction.

Clutching his purchases, he left, without so much as a sideways glance. Sarah's disappointment was complete. But she ordered and waited as the shopkeeper went out the back to get the right change. Finally, as she left with her own afternoon treats, who should still be outside the shop but Siggy, having added to his culinary fare with a steaming bag of dim-sims from the fish and chip shop next door.

"May as well walk with you," he ventured, and slipped into step with Sarah as they headed off in the same direction. Sarah was flustered, shocked and delighted, temporarily unable to speak. Fortunately, Siggy smoothed the awkwardness by pushing the brown paper bag towards her.

"You like dim sims?"

Maybe after all these years, she would have forgotten this first, significant moment of youthful infatuation with a boy her own age. But there it all was recorded in the neat handwriting in the little diary.

Siggy offered me one of his dim-sims!

Next to this entry three hearts were drawn in red biro.

Sarah felt herself flush, reading her adolescent writing. How pathetic, she thought.

And here was another memory she had quite forgotten.

Mr Robb had a car accident last week. Thank heavens he's out of hospital and ok now. It seems the class essays were in the back seat and some of his blood made its way to the papers. When he gave the essays back we were all pretty excited to see who had more blood on their essay.

Arghh! How bizarre, she thought. In these Covid days no one would be wanting any sort of bodily fluids from anyone else on anything they owned. Skimming ahead several pages, she found even more cause for mortification.

Dreamt of Mr Robb last night. He was kissing me and running his hands all over me. I felt all hot and nervous. He is so gorgeous. I want to marry someone like him one day.

Always the older ones — they were the men she cast her eyes upon. In primary school it had been Mr Kelly, her 4th grade teacher. She'd even had a photo of him stuck to the wall above her bed. The man was ancient, probably at least 40, beginning to go bald, so he surely must have been some sort of father figure substitute.

Ah yes, the father again. Her mind strayed to the man she loved, but had a level of contempt for, at the same time.

Chapter 3

London 1935 – Harry practises
all manner of things

Harry Herschcovitch was feeling very agitated. His mother was giving him a hard time.

Harry had started learning violin at the age of five, and had shown much promise. He had a natural talent for music, so, after buying him his first violin, his parents had great ambitions for their precious son. It was easy for him to gain acceptance to the prestigious London Guild Hall School of Music at age eighteen, after his high school years finished. And being such a prized student meant he had a chance to avoid the fate of many young men of his age who worked in some dull job, with only the prospect of a pedestrian work-life stretching out before them.

It was early September and the school had just broken up for the autumn holiday. Harry had been looking forward to taking things a bit easy, staying home, while also putting some hours into practising that Kreisler violin concerto for the end of year concert. Even better, he looked forward to maybe indulging himself in a bit of a good time with Beth, the family's upstairs/downstairs maid.

Beth had been his very precocious introduction to the joys of sex at the unlikely age of thirteen. Five years his senior, she had happily inducted the young lad into carnal pleasures and it made a pleasant escape from the drudgery of her working life. It set a course for him in life that he never veered far from – women were there for his pleasure and seemed very keen to grant it to him.

"Herschl," his mother said ominously in heavily accented English, "you must be sure you be ready for the end of year concert. You need to practise more hours every day. Please, you go now and make two hours violin before we are eating."

So, Kreisler was in, Beth definitely out, at least for the moment.

Months passed during which he practised incessantly, and at times resentfully, driven by his ambitious parents. They had come from modest backgrounds, his mother Betsy from somewhere in Poland and his father Meyer from a small Transylvanian town in Romania.

After emigrating to England, Meyer had briefly made good in business as a furrier, but he had lost much of it in some shady black market dealings during World War I. Now Meyer and Betsy transferred their hopes to their oldest child, the golden boy Harry. His two sisters, Rose and Phyllis, were lucky to escape the burden of their parents' expectations.

"You will be a great violin player – as good as Menuhin," his mother told him with alarming and disconcerting regularity. "But you got to practise! More hours! Every day."

Promising Pupils.

A sure sign of the end of the season is the number of pupils' concerts, sources of more or less anxiety to their teachers and of little interest to the public yet forming a very important part of every artist's development. At the Guild-hall School of Music on Wednesday Miss Phyllis Doreen Simons and Mr. Harry Hershcovitch gave a pianoforte and violin recital and played in a manner that attested to their individual talent and careful teaching. Miss Simons has a sympathetic touch and considerable executive facility, and should do well. Mr Herschcovitch is more advanced. His tone was good, his attack firm, and his readings manly.

A London newspaper reviews students' performances

Young Harry with his older sister

Chapter 4
Time to settle down

Harry had been a gangly little boy, but had grown into quite a good-looking youth, and now in his early twenties, his piercing blue eyes contrasting with his swarthy complexion made him someone the women seemed to notice.

But, despite the attention of various women at school and in the local community, he could always feel his mother's disapproval boring into him.

"Herschl, you will never be playing so good as Menuhin if you don't practise more. Too much time spent chasing girls, and what no-good girls they are. You need to be thinking from marrying a good Jewish girl, my son."

Harry had been a student for three years now at the Guild Hall School of Music in London. His tutors were impressed with his talent, if a little concerned that he was always a bit too much of the show pony, pushing himself forward, never managing to sit comfortably, unobtrusively even, which made him rather troublesome as a member of the school orchestra. His style of playing always included extra flourishes, extravagant sweeps of the bow, and a concentrated scowl that he no doubt thought made him look like a very serious musician. Nevertheless, hopes were now high, not only from his parents, but also from his teachers, that he might in fact make it to the top. If only he would settle down to a more rigorous routine and stop all the chasing of women.

"Perhaps you could give me some private tuition," Harry suggested one day to his music theory teacher, Mona de Fevre, a tall leggy brunette who was gossiped about among

Meyer and Betsy Herschcovitch

her students for having married a much older man some years ago. Her husband Jacques was renowned as a fine violinist and was often away from home, touring the concert hall circuit. It seemed Mona had a soft spot for violinists!

"I just can't seem to grasp some of these finer points, and you are so skilled in this area." Harry eyed her lasciviously, just a hint of a smile playing upon his lips, his delicate, precious hands gesturing in an appeal to her altruistic instincts.

Poor Mona didn't stand a chance. Harry played her like a fine instrument, visiting twice weekly. Just who taught who was a moot point.

The day Jacques returned home from his tour unexpectedly was one Harry would never forget. Reclining exhausted in Mona's large four-poster bed, he was fantasising about what to eat for dinner, and whether he could go another round with Mona, when abruptly the door opened. The large frame of Jacques loomed for a moment, before the shocked husband hurled himself at Harry, bellowing at the top of his lungs.

"Mon Dieu! What in the name of God is going on here – get out, get out – both of you!"

The ensuing scandal cost Mona her job and nearly lost Harry his place at the esteemed school.

"Herschl, what should we do with you!" exclaimed his mother in despair.

Never one to let a chance go by and to remedy a potentially precarious situation, Betsy soon became a one-woman matchmaking service for her son. Each month she hosted afternoon teas with local Jewish families, inviting any eligible daughters along. They came in all shapes and sizes, batting their eyelashes and cooing over Harry like mournful doves. He remained steadfastly unimpressed.

Until one afternoon, Rose Liebovitch and her parents came to visit. She was a little older than Harry, had the dark looks and bold features he loved, and to his surprise, was apparently a talented piano student at another well-known London music school.

Their initial shy meeting, Rose with eyes lowered to avoid Harry's eyes roaming across her voluptuous body, soon led to afternoons in which they would play music together, entertaining both sets of parents with finely executed violin and piano duets.

Betsy kept an eagle eye on Harry, keen that he did not launch into any inappropriate activities with Rose, and put her off him. Champing at the bit to indulge his fantasies with this lovely woman, Harry finally decided the time was right and proposed. The parents were all delighted as the young couple headed for the *chupah* at their local synagogue.

The wedding was an extravagant affair, with nearly a hundred guests, plenty of fine food, drink and merriment, along with a lively band playing a mix of Jewish tunes and the latest popular songs. Even the bride and groom entertained their guests with a couple of musical duets.

~~~

Marriage to Rose was more than he could have hoped for. She was a strong-willed woman, but gentle, loving and kind, and it seemed for a while the little home they had set up could be the salvation of Harry. He was still pursuing his studies, playing concerts and doing orchestra work where he could get it, while Rose juggled home-making duties with teaching piano.

After three years of marriage and eager to start a family, Rose raised the issue with Harry one night.
~~~

"Darling, our studies are over, we're earning plenty. Wouldn't it be nice to have a baby?"

"No, no, just not possible with all our other commitments at the moment," Harry emphatically declared, barely giving it a moment's thought. "Besides, Mother and Father are giving us tickets for that trip to New York. Who knows, I may get a musical engagement over there. That has to be number one priority."

Rose swallowed her disappointment, ever eager to please her talented husband.

Harry marries Rose

Chapter 5
July 1939 – The Big Apple

Ocean-going liners always smacked of exoticness, romance and a bit of mystery. So it was with great excitement that Harry and Rose put their lives on hold for a couple of months, and boarded the luxury liner the *Queen Mary*, sailing from Southampton, London to New York.

Despite the growing rumblings of war in Europe, the holiday was a blessed escape from the routines of life for the young couple. The pressures of teaching, playing, running a house, even of their parents' not-so-subtle nagging ("When are you two going to start a family, give us some grandchildren?") were momentarily left behind.

The luxurious liner was something they could have only ever dreamed of. The ship looked as if it had emerged from a movie set with huge sweeping staircases with polished bannisters, velvet-covered armchairs, crisp white linen on tables decked with gleaming cutlery and elegant gold-rimmed, fine china plates.

The entertainment was something Harry and Rose looked forward to each night, starting at 9 pm. The ship's orchestra played a selection of tunes and then various talented passengers performed solos.

"And now," announced the MC, Mrs Rose Herschcovitch will play 'Consolation' by Liszt."

Rose's hands teased the keyboard into melodic delights, and she finished the piece to rapturous applause.

"And now Mrs Herschcovitch's husband Harry will play

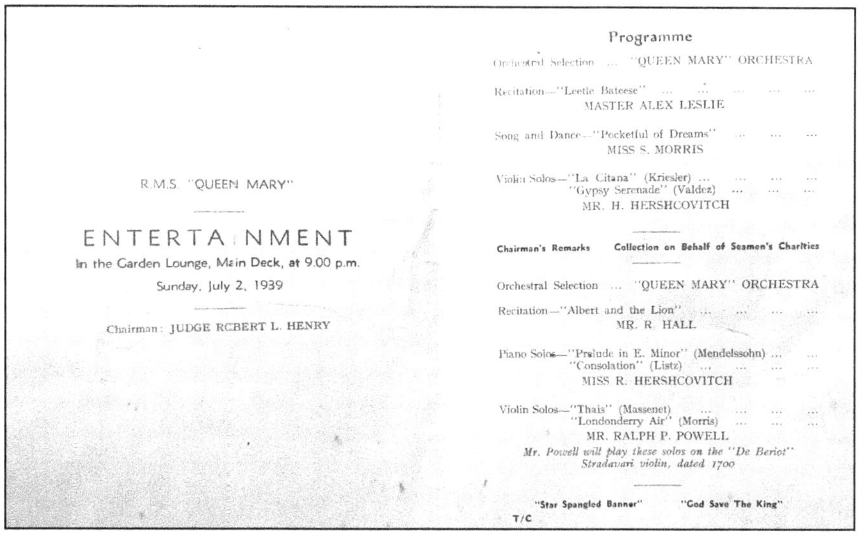

Harry and Rose perform in the evening concert
on the *Queen Mary*

on the violin 'Las Gitana' by Kreisler." Harry took to the podium, the trademark earnest frown on his face, violin tucked beneath cocked head, cushioned by a scrunched up old white handkerchief. There was no denying his virtuosity and the clear notes rang out, but there was something almost ostentatious about him, bringing more attention to himself rather than the music. Still, the audience were once more in raptures, especially the women casting admiring glances at his handsome features.

Surprisingly, four days into the voyage, Rose began suffering horrific seasickness, causing her to retire to their cabin.

To his own surprise, Harry felt a sudden sense of freedom. Here was a chance to spend a little time alone, without the albeit wonderful wife who had been constantly at his side for three years now.

That night Harry once more played a solo during the entertainment hour on the ship.

"Mr Violinist!" An American accent rang out across the room. "Can you play 'Someone to Watch Over Me'?" The request came from a young woman seated at a table of eight, the men dressed in expensive-looking suits, the women in glittering gowns and sporting a goodly range of sparkling jewellery.

Flattered and emboldened by the request, Harry left the podium and sauntered over to the table. His bowing technique had never been better as his hands moved precariously close to the low decolletage neckline of the porcelain-skinned blonde who had so audaciously called out the request. She fluttered her artificial eyelashes at him.

As the tune ended, a man at the table slipped a pound note into Harry's top pocket, while the blonde surreptitiously managed to slip a scrap of paper into Harry's trouser pocket, unseen by the rest of her entourage.

Feeling a sense of guilt, Harry decided he'd better check in with his nausea-stricken wife.

"How did it go darling?" Rose asked weakly from her sick bed.

"Terrific, really good. Audience loved me."

He looked contemplatively at his wife for a moment before announcing, "I really don't think I can sleep yet. A bit too wound up. Do you mind awfully if I just take the air on deck for a while. I'll sneak in so as not to wake you. Hopefully you'll be asleep soon."

Kissing her lightly on the forehead, he made his way to a cabin on the deck above, clutching the piece of paper the blonde had put into his pocket.

Fun in New York

She opened the door dressed in a sheer negligee, her previously upswept hair now flowing over her shoulders.

"Quickly!" She pulled him into the cabin. "My husband has joined his friends in the cigar room and should be gone for at least an hour. Let's not waste it."

Harry didn't have to be asked twice. There was a restlessness in him that no one woman seemed able to quell.

Chapter 6
1939 – The world at war

Harry's anticipation of finding work in New York was soon to be squashed. The answers were the same everywhere. Too much uncertainty in the world to be hiring new musicians for this club or that restaurant.

After several weeks, they returned to their little London apartment and the humdrum of daily life. Except it was less and less humdrum by the day, as the political situation in the country became more and more fraught and tensions between England and Germany mounted.

On the fateful evening of September 3, after rehearsal with the local orchestra, Harry decided to drop in on his parents. Rose had stayed at home, tutoring a prize piano student.

His parents seemed more agitated than usual.

"Come, come, bubeleh, sit with us and listen," insisted Betsy.

Together with his father, the three sat listening to the voice of their prime minister Neville Chamberlain, loud but crackly, coming over BBC radio.

He began with the words, "I am speaking to you from the Cabinet Room at 10 Downing Street. This morning the British Ambassador in Berlin handed the German Government a final note stating that unless we heard from them by 11 o'clock that they were prepared at once to withdraw their troops from Poland, a state of war would exist between us. I have to tell you now that no such undertaking has been received, and that consequently this country is at war with Germany."

The Prime Minister continued, but Harry and his parents barely registered the rest of the five-minute speech. They were in a state of shock, wondering what the implications of this were, for Harry in particular.

It was a month later that all men between the ages of twenty-one and twenty-three were required to enlist.

In August 1940, when he could no longer avoid the fate of being called up, Harry reluctantly stowed his violin in its case and mentally steeled himself to the next six months' training with the Royal Air Force.

The night before he left, Rose was beside herself. Her beloved husband had become emotionally more distant since they returned from New York, and now a huge wedge would be put between them, as he lived life stationed somewhere far away from her. Despite knowing Harry had no choice in the matter, Rose felt somehow abandoned.

"You promise to write?" she pleaded, eyes welling with tears.

"Yes, of course my love, of course." The charm he could so easily turn on for women came to the fore. "Come, let's not waste our last night together." He led her by the hand to their bedroom.

~~~

At first Harry was on clerical duties on the ground. He could do this job with ease, and soon became bored. He decided to volunteer to become a member of aircrew under the auspices of Bomber Command. To be accepted, he had to sit an exam with much emphasis upon maths, which, along with music, was another of Harry's strong points.

He passed with flying colours and was sent to train further to be a wireless operator in bombers. That training also proved relatively easy for him, although learning Morse Code presented a challenge at times.
~~~

While training, he and a group of three other young men were billeted out with local families in Blackpool. It felt like a brief moment of normality, and Harry revelled in his time in a home away from barracks, not least because the family had a stunning eighteen-year-old daughter, Eliza, with whom he quickly bonded.

Finally, training was over; all the young men were declared war-ready and sent by train north, to be stationed with a squadron in Yorkshire.

Training had proved surprisingly good fun for Harry, who had acquitted himself well, even coming to believe that war was actually quite a lark. But when the time finally came to take to the skies, it was another matter.

"We're heading to Germany tomorrow, lads," the commanding officer instructed the crew of seven men at breakfast one morning. "Our bomb load with be 88 thirty-pound incendiaries and 995 four-pounders. Be ready for take-off at 19.30 hours."

Harry felt his stomach stir with nervous anticipation. So, this was the real thing.

"Hey Paddy, old chum, so we're finally going," he said to his fellow crew member sitting next to him. The taciturn Irishman simply grunted, and continued shovelling a rasher of bacon, perched on a doorstep of toast, into his mouth.

Harry felt his appetite suddenly wane, but he gulped down the bitter camp coffee anyway, with an added spoon of powdered milk.

One hour before take-off, the seven-man crew set about readying themselves, donning heavy fur-collared leather bomber jackets and running final checks. The sun had long set and a chill was in the air as the men clambered into the Stirling idling on the runway. With a roar of engines, the lumbering beast became airborne and headed east towards Germany.

Harry had never felt so scared in his life. He could feel his heart rate accelerate, and his bowels rumble ominously. Taking his seat behind the pilot and next to the navigator, he put on the headphones in readiness for taking radio orders from the base.

The journey over the Channel and into enemy territory seemed to take forever and he grew progressively colder. Had he not been engaged in communication with base, Harry felt he could have passed out from sheer terror. When the plane finally arrived over the target area, he was petrified the search lights would illuminate their aircraft and they'd be shot down.

As the bomb aimer announced it was time for the drop, the heavy load was released. The men could see vast areas of ground below illuminated by orange and red flames, like something out of hell. Their plane, relieved of its load, lurched upwards, but the adept pilot ducked, dived and immediately turned for home. Luck had been with Harry on the first bombing run of his air force career.

The next run a week later saw his crew not so lucky. The plane was halfway across the Channel, returning to England, when its left engine started sputtering. Harry felt the chilling fear envelop him as his brain whirred with thoughts of imminent death. His body went rigid as the plane limped its way back to English soil. The men let out a unanimous cheer when the aircraft landed with a screech and a thump.

That night Harry drank half a bottle of whisky to calm his fear of mortality.

The following morning, hungover but glad to be alive, Harry took his usual place at the breakfast trestle. Looking at the now familiar faces, he saw that one of the young radio operators from another squadron wasn't there.

"Where's good ol' Jimmy?" he asked another airman.

"Poor bastard's plane took a hit last night," was the curt reply.

Harry felt once more clammy fear prickling up his neck.

How does a person cope with the daily imminent threat of death? Harry couldn't fathom it. The brave ones, as he thought of some of his squadron mates, just get on with it, try not to think too deeply, and do what must be done.

A good Jewish family, such as the one Harry grew up in, didn't tend to drink a lot of alcohol. Maybe the odd shot of some serious spirit here and there to celebrate a wedding or a bar mitzvah. Harry, unaccustomed to drinking in his youth, was rapidly becoming used to it, if only as a coping strategy.

One night, having just been granted a weekend's leave, he was sitting in a bar with Paddy, the rear gunner from his squadron. He knew he should already be on his way back to Rose, waiting for him in their apartment, but other things seemed to be calling to him.

"Ah Harry, me matey, have yourself a shot. It'll do you a power of good," urged Paddy, as he downed his third generous glass of straight whisky. "Let's get ourselves well and truly pickled and see what the local lasses have to offer."

Despite feeling a modicum of guilt, Harry had already checked out what the local lasses had to offer. His wayward encounter on the cruise liner had awakened a taste in him for fleshly delights other than those offered by his wife.

~~~

Sarah had loved hearing Harry's stories over the breakfast table, when she was a little girl.

"Daddy, tell me about the time the other plane exploded," she cajoled.
~~~

And Harry regaled her grisly young imagination with the tale of how, one night, he and his crew were sitting on the runway, all set for take-off, when the Lancaster up ahead of them suddenly exploded. The fireball would leave not one crew member alive.

Over Harry's wireless came the instruction, "G for George, you're next to take off." War had no respect for men's fears.

"Daddy, now tell me about how they used to have to hose the rear gunner out of the plane after you came back from a bombing mission."

And she listened with rapt attention to the details her father somehow managed to make exciting. Perhaps that was where she got her taste for grisly serial killer murder novels!

"Daddy, why did you change your name from Herschcovitch during the war?"

"If my plane had been shot down," her father replied, "I would have been a sitting duck to be carted off to the concentration camps, with such an obviously Jewish name."

Sarah thought how extraordinary life must have been during those war years. You'd live for the day, for the moment, constantly fearful, frequently relieved and celebrating with alcohol, always part of a surreal living hell. How could she possibly think her life had anything so troubling as to compare with what her parents had been through?

She remembered too how Harry had cowered under the kitchen table whenever a thunderstorm hit Melbourne. At the time she had thought it a lark, something he did to appeal to her childish sense of humour. She hadn't heard of post-traumatic stress disorder in those days. Looking back, it made sense.

Chapter 7
1970 – First love

Sarah continued her fossicking, at once intrigued and mortified by the many long-forgotten experiences from her teenage years, all written about in embarrassing details in her various diaries. At the bottom of the fruit box was a particular diary, held closed by a little brass lock, certainly no match for any prying eyes that wanted access.

As she began to read, Sarah was transported back to her first year at university – carefree times, yet also days of promise and hope, with an entire life to look forward to, but for now a breathing space somewhere between the world of adolescence and adulthood.

Sarah's mother Angela was a loving but strict parent. The two had an unnaturally close relationship, with perhaps too many secrets inappropriate for a mother to confide in her daughter. But Sarah was no longer a little girl and Angela, recognising that her daughter needed more freedom, now reluctantly let her go to the occasional party, but always with exhortations about the time she must be home, and never to come home with anyone except Jen and Keith, who would be allowed to drive her there.

The end of term university party was the night she met Richard, the man who would eventually become her first *grand amour*, her first sexual partner. He caught her eye across the room, mostly because he was the most handsome man there, slightly built, and sort of Bohemian looking, in his suede jacket. After they got to talking in the kitchen she realised he was not only good-looking, but smart, warm and funny.

"Hi," he ventured as they both made a beeline for the cask of cheap moselle. "I'm Ricardo. Well, people generally call me Richy. And you are?"

"Sarah," she responded, flustered that this handsome fellow should even be bothered speaking to her.

"So what's your story? Third year? Let me guess – science/engineering?"

"Nothing so grand," responded Sarah, "though I did finish a science HSC at high school. Wanted to do psychology, but got so sick of algebra and applied maths, I took the easy path and swapped to an arts degree. It's sort of more human and interesting."

She learned that Richy was aiming for a teaching qualification, two years ahead of her in his studies. Before long, they veered off the safe topic of studies and started comparing their backgrounds and families. Surprisingly, Richy came from Italian heritage, two generations back, and his family were still very connected to the "old country", with just a few of them having immigrated to Melbourne.

Sarah liked that he was not your average Aussie bloke – with her background, she felt somehow more comfortable with anyone of a background that she didn't perceive as ocker.

Despite her mother's exhortations that she return home with Jen and Keith, she accepted Richy's invitation to be driven home by him.

"Oh! I've never ridden in a sports car!" she exclaimed, as he helped her into the passenger seat of his British racing-green, low-slung Austin-Healey Sprite.

Her excitement turned to trepidation and fear of her mother's wrath when, halfway home, the Sprite spluttered and abruptly ground to a halt.

"Oh shit! Sorry," Richy burst out. "These things are notoriously temperamental."

Fortunately Richy was a sensible type and had a membership with the RACV, so they had the pleasure of a tow-truck ride home.

They clambered up into the high truck, feeling both foolish and exhilarated.

"Oh gosh!" exclaimed Sarah. "I hope my mother doesn't kill me."

"You'll be okay," said Richy, patting her knee in a way that sent an electric jolt through her body. The driver first swung by Sarah's house, then carted Richy and the Sprite away.

Luckily, Sarah's mother chose to either ignore her daughter's late return, or was genuinely asleep. Scrambling into bed, Sarah found she couldn't sleep, so she got up and turned on the night light to find her precious diary.

She poured her heart out – insecure ramblings, indicating that she was almost too scared to hope her attraction to Richy would turn out to be something. They seemed to have clicked together and yet, suppose he never called? Suppose they began to date, and then after a couple of weeks of going out it would probably all come to an abrupt end. That old gremlin of potential rejection was waiting around the corner to jump out and get her again.

What if it ended like it had with that lovely boy she'd dated when she was in her last year of high school? He'd been older than she was, and obviously expected much more than she was able to give, especially with her mother keeping an eagle eye upon the two of them.

But two weeks after meeting, she and Richy were going steady, and a month later she'd lost her virginity in the back seat of a car.

<div style="text-align:center">~~~</div>

Leafing through the old diary, Sarah was almost embarrassed at the outpouring of love, desire and obsession that was in her writings. She had truly forgotten what it was like to experience that first love in one's life. After all the foolish high school crushes, all the unsuitable boys who she'd fumbled with in back seats of cars, here was someone totally quite different – mature, and simply gorgeous. Many of her writings expressed the fear that Richy would lose interest in her and break up with her, but he seemed genuinely keen from the outset.

Yet what a disappointment her first full-on sexual encounter had been; she felt nothing – no pain, no pleasure, just an invasive sensation, so unremarkable that she asked Richy, "Is that really what sex is?". Laughingly, he assured her it was.

To Sarah's complete surprise, her mother decided the time was ripe to let her off the leash. What brought about this dramatic change, Sarah would never grasp.

"You're eighteen now. You're grown up. Maybe you want to invite Richy over for tea? Dad will be out working and I've got a theatre group party," she said, the implications being clear. "And by the way, maybe it's time to get yourself put on the pill."

One year later, Sarah and Richy were engaged and set to be married, much to the slight consternation of both their mothers. For Sarah it was a wonderful prospect that she would finally escape the cloying situation in her home – the endless focus of her mother's attention and the ceaseless sniping war between her parents. Of late, the sniping was escalating to something that felt more serious; all the more reason to make a hasty escape.

Rosa, Richy's mother, was a kind-hearted woman who, herself, had married at the age of sixteen. On the phone to Angela, she articulated those reservations.

"You know how much I love Sarah, we all do, but she's so young. Do you really think she is ready for marriage? Does she know what she's getting into?"

"I try to tell her," Angela countered, "but she's determined. Let's hope they'll be happy. With Richy being older, he might be able to help her grow up."

By the time they married, Sarah was still only a third-year uni student. Richy had started his teaching, so their life was a juggle between studies, work, and of course plenty of socialising with friends.

Her new husband's school posting was in an outer suburb, which could almost be considered semi-rural. They started their married life renting a small apartment, but were soon able to graduate to a modest house, replete with a tiny garden and a cat.

Sarah's first sexual experience had perhaps set the tone for her later life. Although Richy was patient and loving, she never seemed to experience great desire or joy in the activity.

"Why do you want to do that?" she asked, "We did that only two weeks ago."

Somewhere in her mind, Richy had become like a grown-up playmate, not the man she had first perceived him as. Perhaps his slight build made her see him as a boy, and combined with his under-endowment of body hair, unusual for an Italian, he seemed even more child-like to her. Not a "real man", hairy and swarthy like her father, or even Mr Robb.

"Let's have a baby," Richy cajoled one night. "I've really wanted to start a family."

Sarah's eyes widened in alarm. "Good God, no way. I'm still a baby myself," she spluttered. "No, no, it's way too soon."

All around her, girlfriends of the same age were starting to create their mandatory families of 2.2 children. But the thought of that terrified her.

By the time she graduated from university, having barely turned twenty-one, and headed off to her first teaching post, Sarah was starting to feel trapped in her marriage. She'd gone from a relatively confined home situation to another domestic life full of obligations – housework, cooking, gardening. Wasn't one supposed to be having fun at this young age?

Her first posting was to a school even further away from the city than Richy's, and there were many first-year out teachers, all young and full of life and frivolity. After school, some of them would head off down to the local pub, where they'd joke, drink, compare notes on the day just passed, and sometimes even stay on, going to the pub for a bite of dinner.

Richy was still teaching by day at a nearby high school. Like Sarah, he was an English teacher, but he'd recently decided he needed to further explore his creative side, and decided to go back to further part-time studies. He often found himself working late with his pals at college, writing up film scripts, or getting together with their makeshift blues band. It meant Sarah no longer had to feel guilty about not coming home to cook dinner.

"You coming, Sarah?" asked Jake, also new to the school, and teaching in the science faculty. He had a boyish, cheeky grin, and his sandy beard gave him the look of an older man, someone a bit fatherly, a bit roguish.

She thought for a moment. Richy would no doubt be with his college pals.

"Sure, why not?" she responded.

The warm embrace of the country pub and a couple of red wines soon made Sarah's head spin. She found herself in easy conversation with Jake, who occasionally stressed a point he made by placing his hand over hers. The frisson of excitement she felt was disturbing, but also seductive.

As the group parted after a cheap and cheerful meal, Jake caught her eye meaningfully.

"See you tomorrow then? – look forward to it." He winked.

The drive home was a long one, down narrow dimly-lit roads, but emboldened by her night, Sarah turned the radio up loud, gunning her little Datsun over the speed limit until, thankfully minus incident, she arrived home.

Surprisingly, Richy was already home and she found herself slightly annoyed. Her indulgent reverie of her evening flirting with Jake was interrupted, even more so because Richy was obviously looking forward to some action with his wife.

Her excuses were immediate. "Oh sorry, Rich, I've drunk too much – maybe tomorrow."

He never pushed the issue. The disappointment on his face told it all, and Sarah was happy enough to snuggle into him, all the while thinking of Jake.

Chapter 8
1976 – Decision crisis

At last Sarah was away from it all – away overseas to Europe for the first time – away from the two men who professed undying love for her. Despite the persuasiveness of both their arguments, she found herself totally unable to make a decision; to go back to her husband of five years, sweet Richy whom she'd married too young, or to make a new life with Jake, the forceful, smooth-talking man who had lured her away from her marriage vows.

Safely ensconced in Athens for five weeks with her oldest friend Roula, she at least didn't have to make any decisions for a while. Hell, she could even cut off and not think about it at all, except for the letters that turned up from each of them like clockwork.

The letters now sat like recriminations from the past. With trembling hands she opened the first one from Richy. The letter was newsy but with a deep underlying sadness. The letter that had started off as news, ended up as an outpouring of grief and sorrow that the girl he loved so much had upped and left.

Richy wrote so beautifully; his use of language and his ability to express deep emotion touched her still, but of course, back then, the girl she'd been had not seen it, let alone appreciated it. Still today, nearly fifty years on, Sarah felt a level of guilt, regret and even mortification at what she had done.

Jake's letters were all about sex, passion and love – if there was indeed much difference between these as far as her relationship with Jake went. He protested that he truly loved her, but it really seemed as if he were driven by feelings that ultimately were little more than sexual.

Sarah had not a clue really as to why she'd left Richy, other than her overwhelming feeling of being trapped, perhaps a bit overshadowed by him, and an irresistible attraction to Jake.

Chapter 9
There is life out there

This lockdown thing was starting to become tedious. How many hours could one spend watching pay TV, or not-pay free to air TV, cleaning cupboards and cooking up new delights?

Sarah marvelled at the creativity of the many musicians who still had the drive to post their efforts on Facebook. Just yesterday she'd stumbled across a song from her past – 'Kyrie Eleison'. During a pandemic you didn't have to be religious to grasp the irony of the words, meaning "Christ Have Mercy on Us". More than that, she was struck forcibly by how incredibly talented each individual musician was, and when they grouped together, connecting over one of those clever programs like Zoom, they absolutely nailed the song. She suddenly found herself in tears for the joy of the achievement, and the loss of the contact that these people must be craving with each other. After all, nothing could beat the high of a band getting together in real life. Even getting a song right over the net could not equal that. Just like no amount of Zooming with friends or with David could make up for the absence of their physical presence.

Then came the grand announcement from the powers that be. The first lockdown was finally lifted – not in a huge way, but people were informed they could go outside, visit local attractions, gather in groups of ten in a park, and even invite five people to their homes. Always somewhat paranoid, Sarah didn't want to jump in too soon. She chose to make a solitary visit to the seaside walking track, not far from her home.

There were many people out and about – kids playing cricket, couples walking hand in hand, youngsters oblivious to the cold, wading up to their knees. Hearing the wheeling cries of the gulls and seeing the world come alive again was overwhelming. All the things one took for granted were there to be appreciated in the moment, and what a moment it was.

Walking back as the sun started its early winter descent mid-afternoon, she was almost shocked by the glimmer of gold and silver strewn across the shallow water. It suddenly seemed to be an incarnation of every lovely moment, every sad moment, every loss and joy in her life. It brought a feeling she could almost taste – that of the many past moments that would never return, moments that took you back in time like opening a bottle of perfume.

She put her earpods in and tuned her phone to a favourite playlist, reflecting that songs, too, were like a bottle of perfume; a portal to the past. So often she heard a song that transported her back to moments in her childhood when she first discovered the radio and the delights of the hit parade. Other songs evoked the teen years of first love and longing. Sometimes, hearing them, she felt a spring in her step, a vague delusion that she was actually young again. Maybe this good-looking jogger going past would look her way … dream on – she was too old for any of that now, and besides, she was married, even if David was stuck half a world away for God knows how long.

~~~

Even though the lockdown was over, the Pandora's box that she had opened up was now irresistible. What had started off as a small clear-up of memorabilia in boxes in the cupboards seemed to be ever expanding. What more was there to be discovered, or rediscovered? In some ways it was a real insight, in others it was doing her head in. Sure,
~~~

reading her old diaries came under the insight category, but why on earth did she have to keep everything? All these old boxes of cards from past lovers, and even those she'd sent to her parents and those from them to her. Letters from every vaguely significant man who had come and gone in her life. Not to mention every photographic negative from the days of analogue cameras and the endless albums of hard copy photos stashed on the bookshelves.

Perhaps the negatives could be disposed of? Sarah hauled the box out. Sticking up from the side of the box was a small photograph that certainly was not in its logical home.

The photo was sepia, with yellowing edges. A young woman smiled shyly out – dark wavy hair, large eyes, well-shaped brows, basically very lovely but something was amiss. She was dressed in an odd sort of 19th century costume. Of course, thought Sarah – it's when her beautiful mother, Angela, had been in the theatre in England, a time when she had escaped her brutal childhood, left her exciting war years, and was making a name for herself in a field where she had apparently shone. It was a time before she'd been dragged away from her life's true passion, diverted by a man in a way that would change her life forever.

Chapter 10
1924–41 – Amazing Grace

Angela had not always been her name. The breech baby that had nearly killed her mother, Elsie, had been christened Grace. Elsie had been married to Walt, a hard-working, unassuming London crane driver who loved to grow over-sized chrysanthemums on his weekends. He had few aspirations, other than to care for his children. Elsie, however, fancied herself as better than a working-class man's wife.

In fact, it seemed that Elsie didn't even want to be a mother, but despite this, when Grace was two, a baby brother Dennis came on the scene. As the children grew, Elsie saw them as little more than nuisances, mouths to feed, endless drains on the household budget. She always wanted more than Walt could give her, especially on his meagre wages.

"Your income just won't do," she sniped. "We'll take in a lodger; that'll bring in a bit more."

When Tom the lodger came to stay in the spare room, life changed irrevocably. Elsie soon took to having afternoon tea with the heavy-set man, leaving Walt and the children to their own devices. While Elsie and the lodger indulged in scones with real butter, Walt and the children ate stale bread, smeared with dripping from the Sunday roast.

Grace noticed how much happier her mother was looking, and it was a relief not to have the evil-tempered woman always in her face. She soon noticed, too, how much fatter her mother was growing.

When the baby was born, it looked remarkably unlike Grace and Dennis. Elsie showered what could only be interpreted

Above: Infant Grace
Below: Sheila, Dennis, Grace

as maternal love on the new infant, Sheila. It meant there was no love left for Grace and Dennis, not that there ever had been much.

Elsie, in fact, grew meaner in spirit to Walt and her two older children. She was given to fits of temper and gave the pair a thrashing on the smallest pretext.

Grace, now almost ten years old, had always loved going to school. It was a welcome escape from home. She was smart and loved to read and at night she sought refuge in books. Finding a precious torch Walt had given her for her previous birthday, Grace huddled under the covers, immersed in a made-up world that went some way to obliterate the pain of the current one.

This was an activity Elsie couldn't tolerate.

"Oh, you think you're little Miss Muck, don't you. Turn out that light now, or you'll see the back of my hand!" Her mother had a way of scolding and being supercilious all at the one time.

Days, weeks and years dragged by with school being Grace's only salvation. But now that she was older and at a secondary school, she could no longer walk there.

One frosty morning, she packed her schoolbag with a meagre jam sandwich and her beloved books.

"Ah, Mum, I'll need that threepence for the bus please."

Elsie was in a fouler mood than usual.

"Who the hell do you think you are, wantin' to study? Think you're better than us all, do you?"

So Grace started the long walk to school, but after weeks of trudging through the slush each day she began to despair. She tried asking her mother again for bus money, but that only made Elsie angrier. On days Elsie got the devil in her, she'd grab the curtain rod and lay into her daughter. "That'll teach you to know your place, you uppity young miss!" she snarled.

By the time Grace reached fourteen, she began to plan her escape. She was confident that she could perhaps make a go of things on her own. Anything would be better than trying to avoid Elsie's sharp tongue and even sharper slaps, or worse.

Anyway, it seemed any semblance of what had once been a family was now in tatters.

Eventually Grace hatched a daring plan. Yes, she would leave home and seek her fortune in the city.

Arriving in central London with only a small battered cardboard case, she soon began to doubt the wisdom of her decision. Where could she go, where would she sleep that night? The meagre coins Walt had given her over the past few months wouldn't go very far. Delaying panic, she tentatively went into a small tea house and ordered a cup of tea, which used up too much of the ten shillings in her pocket.

At a neighbouring table two elegant-looking women were speaking loudly about the problem of finding good help in these troubled times.

The darker haired woman said, "She just upped and left, the cheeky minx. Now who's going to mind the children?"

Grace summoned all her courage and her sweetest smile.

"Excuse me, m'am. I couldn't help but overhear you. I'm looking for work and I just love children."

After giving Grace the once-over, the lamenting woman spoke in an official, but not unfriendly tone.

"How old are you?"

Thinking on her feet, Grace responded quickly, "Just turned seventeen, ma'am."

"Oh well, we are a bit desperate, so why not give it a go. You'll work for free for the first week, then if we like you, it'll be two and sixpence, plus meals and a room after that. What do you say?"

Grace could barely contain her excitement at this fortuitous turn of fate. Her next three years were set in motion.

They were years she barely spoke about later in her life, perhaps uneventful, perhaps ghastly. Sarah would never come to know what her mother's life had been like in that interim period before all hell broke loose in the form of World War Two.

"Oh, goody, a war," exclaimed Grace to one of her fellow workers in "the great house", as they called it. "I'm going to sign up as soon as I turn seventeen!"

"But you need to be eighteen," her friend had declared.

"Then I'll put my age up!" Grace was desperate for a change in her now drab life.

As suddenly as she had left her childhood home, she departed from her lowly employment as nanny and maid, and headed into what she hoped would be a new and exciting phase of life.

Chapter 11
1941 – Grace goes to war

The Anti-Aircraft Command was under the operational direction of the RAF Fighter Command. Various divisions were stationed all around different parts of Britain, from Scotland to Wales, from London to Newcastle.

Despite her lack of formal education, Grace proved a surprisingly good student and, after her initial training, was assigned to the job of spotter with the Auxiliary Territorial Services (ATS). Although not on the front line, the many women in these positions were invaluable to the war effort, lining up enemy targets, plotting courses, and doing much of the groundwork that would see London anti-aircraft artillery repel or shoot down German bombers over London.

Even as a child, Grace had always had a beautiful face, so innocent-looking and now a magnet for men. Though they lusted after her, she generally kept her distance, but this did not preclude making good platonic friendships with some of the men stationed near her. One of her co-officers, Peter Starnowski, used to accompany her to the pub when they were together on leave from military duties.

"Cor, she's a looker your gal!" the admiring soldiers would say.

"She is. She's a looker and a drinker," retorted Peter in a broad Cockney accent that belied his Polish surname. "Tell ya what, I'll bet ya a quid she can drink ya under the table."

"What, her? No bloody way!"

The incredulous gamblers would always take the bet, and

leave with their pockets lighter, as Grace easily lived up to the reputation Peter had spruiked.

Some nights Grace and her fellow army "gals" headed out to the local dance hall, where American soldiers went en masse to drink, dance and hopefully pick up a sweet-faced English lass for the night. It was on just such a night that Grace met Chuck, a smooth-talking handsome Yankee soldier.

"Hey sweetie, you wanna dance?" The words rolled off his tongue like honey, the accent alluring. He extended his hand to Grace who eagerly followed him onto the dance floor. The place was redolent of smoke and the pungent sweat of frenetic dancers doing the jitterbug. Glen Miller was all the rage and 'In the Mood' had the dancers in a frenzy, with the women twirling and jumping, spinning and sweating. But then the band up on stage changed the pace and began to play 'Moonlight Serenade'. Chuck pulled Grace close and began to whisper sweet endearments in her ear. It was all so new for her. Despite being now well beyond her youthful adolescence, she'd never been close to a man and, while it felt somehow dangerous, there was also an allure and excitement about it.

So when Chuck talked her into going with him to a squalid little hotel room, she followed, curiosity mingling with apprehension. Thanks to her total lack of intimate experience, Grace was left perplexed after Chuck pushed her onto the bed, roughly removed her knickers, thrust himself inside her, and after a few grunts rolled off her and fell asleep. Oh, if that's what it's all about, she mused, maybe I can do without it. It was a night to remember, and yet not.

More than her ability to attract men and to drink them under the table, Grace also discovered she had a talent for acting, joining a small military theatrical group. Her enthusiasm for

Grace joins the
war effort

the activity mounted with every performance the group put on and she began to realise that here was where her life's passion lay.

But first there was a war to get through. It had become apparent that Germany was losing the war, but trauma was still all around her. One weekend, she was making her way back to visit her father, who had now separated from Elsie and lived in a tiny bedsit. As she made her way through the devastated streets, Grace spotted a small boy lying among the ruins of a bombed-out building, clutching a teddy bear. Trouble was, the child had no head.

That same weekend, having arrived at her father's home, she fell into an exhausted sleep, and woke to find shattered glass all over her, and a window frame around her head. At least she had had a much needed, decent night's sleep. The extraordinary had become everyday.

Chapter 12

1943 – Harry can't take it any more

Harry had just completed his third bombing mission. Things had gone okay with the drop of the payload, but on returning home, the plane's left engine had failed and the Sterling had limped home, all the men on board fearful that this could be it for them that night.

Harry's hands started to tremble and he felt again the paralysing fear that always assailed him when he heard of the many planes that came to grief. Only when the wounded aircraft finally landed did he breathe a sigh of relief, but vowed to visit the RAF doctor next morning. Perhaps tablets to calm his nerves?

"You're a total wreck, Sergeant Hurst. Your blood pressure is sky-high, your weight is dropping, and you seem to have developed a tremor in your hands. Look, old chap, I'll put in a recommendation that you be transferred to a less stressful job."

Amazingly, it was decided to ship Harry out to India, a country where the British Raj still held sway, and where His Majesty's Government had stationed many troops.

Harry couldn't believe his good fortune. A lucky escape, yet again. But first he needed to pay the obligatory visit back to Rose, as he had done intermittently over the past few years of his war service. Things had been somewhat distant between them, but Harry, ever driven by lustful longings, always took the opportunity to slip into bed with his wife, even though he had plenty of other adventures outside of the marital bed.

After three nights back home with his wife, Harry felt things had perhaps thawed a little between them. In fact, it was almost a little like their early days of courting, except with a lot more sex thrown in. Harry felt great. He'd had a good time. Whether Rose had or hadn't he didn't bother to enquire.

As he kissed her goodbye, heading for the docks, he said cheerily, "I've left you a few pounds under the pillow. Be a good girl and try not to spend it all at once."

And then he was on a ship steaming its way towards India.

By late September 1944, Harry found himself in Delhi, again working as a radio operator, but this time with his feet safely on solid ground. Every military man had been issued with a little book titled 'Some useful hints for soldiers arriving in India'. As well as a basic compendium of useful words in Hindi, it had tips for taking care of one's health. Among them were:

> *Don't go into the blazing sun without your helmet.*
>
> *Don't sleep without a mosquito curtain.*
>
> *Be careful about eating fruit that has been cut or left exposed.*
>
> *Don't lose your head, heart or sleep in India; nor get homesick. The time will pass soon and the handkerchiefs waving adieu at Southampton Quay will seem only yesterday. INDIA IS A FINE COUNTRY AFTER ALL!*

Whether fine or not, India was like nothing he had ever imagined. The crush of people, the sights, the sounds, the colours and smells were all overwhelming. He soon grew to love the sounds of the local peddler crying: "*Chai Wallah*" as he wheeled his drum of steaming sweet tea, redolent of cardamom, into the streets to sell to passers-by.

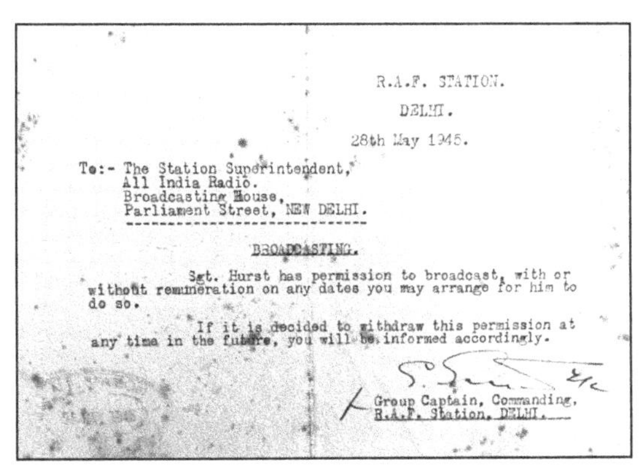

R.A.F. STATION.

DELHI.

28th May 1945.

To:- The Station Superintendent,
All India Radio.
Broadcasting House,
Parliament Street, NEW DELHI.

BROADCASTING.

Sgt. Hurst has permission to broadcast, with or without remuneration on any dates you may arrange for him to do so.

If it is decided to withdraw this permission at any time in the future, you will be informed accordingly.

Group Captain, Commanding,
R.A.F. Station, DELHI.

The heavily fragrant food, laced with an often unbearable amount of chilli, was a far cry from the Polish Jewish fare he'd grown up with. Harry found himself often suffering bouts of dysentery and being send to the military hospital in the high country in northern India for a spot of recuperation.

One evening Harry's commanding officer approached him.

"Sergeant, old chap, listen here. There's one of those local nawab chappies holding a party, and he is keen to have a live musician. I know you've been playing a spot of fiddle on the local radio, so how about we organise a meeting with him, and maybe you can be the entertainment for the night."

And so Harry was introduced to that rarefied Indian air where the extravagantly rich rulers lived. At first the contrast was shocking to him. The poor were so downtrodden, and the rich were so ostentatious, self-indulgent and heedless of the suffering outside their doors. Maharajas who lauded it over the peasants lived in palaces bedecked with more precious jewels that one could imagine possible. They threw parties the likes of which near-starving peasants couldn't begin to imagine, with platters overflowing with food, and any type of alcohol your heart desired.

It didn't take long for Harry to fit into the rhythm of this life, so when he wasn't doing his clerical duties for the RAF or recovering from dysentery, he was stealing the limelight at sumptuous parties, and sometimes stealing the heart of a sari-bedecked Indian memsahib as well.

Even though the British still ruled India, it would be only a couple of years before the country asserted its independence and kicked the conquering Poms out. Meantime, those lucky enough to swan about with the upper echelons of Indian society, like Harry, milked it for all it was worth.

He didn't think too much about Rose back home. Once every few months he was granted leave to return to England. Several months after one such visit, back in India he received a telegram from Rose saying simply: 'You're going to be a daddy'. Harry wasn't sure how he felt about this, so calmed his agitation by a serious bout of drinking, then stripping off his uniform and playing the violin naked under the window of the wife of his commanding officer.

Luckily the officer didn't awake, but the wife, opening the window, was simultaneously charmed and shocked.

"Oh, go back to your barracks, you rude man!" she hissed at him, internally chuckling. Barracks were definitely not on his agenda and, after dressing, easily slipping out past the guard, Harry made his way to a nearby establishment where the local beauties could help ease his anxiety at the thought of having to take responsibility for another little life, and maybe becoming trapped forever.

Harry had to admit however, that the time in India was easier than his short and traumatic stint in bombers. The three years flew past, and were punctuated with letters from Rose, each one featuring a picture of a sweet little curly-headed girl, with captions saying things like 'Mummy says I'm your new pin-up girl'. If only Rose knew how many other pin-up girls her husband had, if not on his wall, in his bed!

~~~

All good things must come to an end, and when the war ended, so did Harry's sojourn in India. He boarded a steamer bound for London, with a vaguely sinking feeling in his heart. Life had been almost fun in the sub-continent, and now he feared he would resume some sort of mundaneness, with a wife and child dominating all, and curtailing his amorous exploits.
~~~

As the troop carrier pulled into Southampton dock, Harry was surprised to see his father standing down below. As the war-weary men spilled onto British soil, Harry approached Meyer.

At first Meyer seemed not to recognise his son. He stepped back apace, and gasped."Oy weh, Herschl, have you been in one of those concentration camps? You are so thin!"

Harry was indeed bordering on skeletal. So many bouts of dysentery and the concomitant recuperation in the Himalayan foothills had certainly taken their toll on his already slight frame.

"Papa, what are you doing here? Where's Rose and my daughter?"

"Big news for you – they have gone to Palestine," Meyer blurted out.

Harry was temporarily dumbstruck. "For God's sake – what on earth!"

"No problem, we get you fattened up a bit, then you go over to meet them." Meyer seemed to have it all figured out.

Chapter 13
Grace chases her dream

When the war finally ended, Grace was demobbed from the army. Now was the time to put her all into pursuing that longed-for career in theatre.

For several weeks she'd been spending her post-service days bunking down on the lumpy sofa of her friend Gillian, an army companion who had the good fortune to have been given a small apartment by her wealthy parents.

Each weekend, Grace and Gillian bought the *London Times* and scoured through it for ideas – for Gillian ideas on social events to attend where she might meet the "right" sort of man, for Grace ideas on where to go next in pursuit of her dream.

An article caught Grace's eye.

"Gillian, look, here's a review of a play that Leicester Theatre Company have just put on. It says at the end they are short of actors and are looking for people to join."

That was it. She knew exactly what to do and where to go.

Leaving the security and safety of London, even though it was so ravaged by war, was an unsettling experience for Grace. Packing her meagre belongings into a battered suitcase, she bid farewell to Gillian and boarded the train north.

The train was packed with men in uniform, which made her feel even more vulnerable and insecure, especially after her tawdry introduction to sex back at the dance hall. In fact, that night with Chuck remained her one and only experience of sex to date.

The Theatre Royal Leicester- home of Leicester
Repertory Group

But her uneasy feelings were soon replaced by excitement and a sense of awe as she fronted up to the grand old building, the Leicester Theatre Royal, the home of the Leicester Repertory Company.

She had telegrammed ahead to say when she would be arriving. There on the steps to the building stood Richard Leacroft, current head of the company. His welcoming smile and warm twinkling eyes put her instantly at ease, as he extended his hand to take her suitcase.

Chapter 14

1946 – Harry heads to Palestine

When Harry arrived in Palestine, the country was a hotbed of political tensions. Since the end of World War I the British had declared their support for setting up a Jewish homeland in Palestine. The Arabs had been none too pleased about this but, as World War II ended and the atrocities of the Holocaust came to light, calls were renewed for a safe Jewish homeland in Palestine.

The day his ship pulled into the port of Haifa, Harry was beset by mixed feelings. His first reaction was to the intense heat. It was a different type of heat from that of India. It was hot and dry, none of that cloying humidity that had troubled him so much over there. Initial impressions were followed by an almost panicky feeling in his gut. It was so strange to be stepping into an instant family.

Down on the dock, he caught sight of the familiar face of his wife, anxiously scanning the decks for a sign of her returned husband. In her arms was a little girl with a head of surprisingly blonde curls. The panic soon evaporated and Harry was eager to see what sort of a child he had created.

Coming down the gangplank he walked towards Rose, and there was an awkward moment before they finally embraced. Pulling away, Harry tickled the cheek of his little daughter, who began immediately to cry.

"She'll get used to you," Rose reassured him. "Oh Harry, I'm so relieved you are safely back with us. But you are so thin! Let's get home and have something to eat. I've cooked your favourites – cabbage rolls and cheesecake."

Maybe this wouldn't be so bad, Harry thought.

The modest apartment in which Rose had lived since coming to Palestine during Harry's absence didn't feel like home to him, the way their London flat had. And though he liked children, Harry found it hard that his small daughter did not seem to be easily getting used to him.

Somehow those years apart had left the young couple more estranged than ever. Harry started to spend as much time as he could away from the family home, either playing violin at the local radio station, or sitting in local coffee shops, cogitating his future.

One day as he sat in the local café, sipping his cardamom-laced coffee, he casually reached for the newspaper. The headlines were shocking. A Zionist movement called the Irgun had set off a bomb in a wing of the King David Hotel in Jerusalem. The hotel was the site of the central offices of the British authorities in Palestine. The Irgun wanted the British out. The terrorist attack had killed more than 90 people, including Brits, Arabs and Jews.

Harry felt as if he had stepped into another kind of, as yet unofficial, war. If Palestine was ever to become a new nation, it seemed there would be much bloodshed and this was not something he felt he could go through again.

Despite the tensions in his marriage, he desperately wanted to get back to England with his wife and daughter. Things were obviously not going to resolve so easily between him and Rose, who was adamant they should stay in this new land, full of hope and promise and, more importantly, acceptance.

They began to fight with alarming regularity, Harry insisting they return to England, Rose saying she loved her new country and did not wish to leave.

Suddenly he had a brainwave. His friend Schmuel at the British Embassy might be able to help.

The next morning Harry donned his hat against the searing sun and made the trek downtown to the Embassy. He hadn't made an appointment, so the officious secretary made him wait for nearly an hour. Finally, Schmuel emerged and ushered him in.

"So Herschl my friend, what brings you here?"

"It's a sad and sorry tale I've come to tell you. In short, I believe my wife Rose is working as an undercover spy for the Irgun. I think it would be in the British interests to deport her back to England."

Schmuel raised his eyebrows sceptically then let out a derisory laugh.

"Rose ... your Rose? My friend, while you have been gone, my wife and I have been lucky enough to share a few meals with your lovely wife, and I'm telling you, there is no way she would be involved in that ugly business. She's as honest as the day is long, and I know she holds no truck for any of those organisations that bring about political ends by violence. Now, if you have nothing further to add, I'm sorry but I'm very busy today."

Schmuel rose from his desk and walked an affronted Harry to the door.

Chapter 15

July 1947 – Harry on the high seas

The ship, RMS *Queen Mary,* had been restored to her former pre-war glory. After being deployed as a troop carrier, she was the recipient of an expensive makeover and looked better than ever.

Harry sat on the deck, pondering the last year or so of his miserable life. His attempt to get Rose expelled from Israel had been a monumental failure. Not only was she popular among the British higher-ups, but Harry's thwarted foray had left him with egg on his face and a sullied reputation.

At parties people whispered behind their hands and cast dark looks his way.

He recalled with anger and shame the night, two days after his visit with Schmuel, that Rose had entered their small kitchen, having put their daughter to bed. She sat down with a thump and a dark look on her face.

She looked Harry square in the face. "What's this I hear from Schmuel's wife about you telling total untruths about me?"

"What are you talking about, dear?" Harry muttered.

"Don't' *dear* me, you can't even tell the truth now. You know, I've had it with you. All those years with the RAF, doing God knows what on your leave. You know the night our daughter was born, your father tried to get in contact with you via his contacts in Bomber Command. There might have been a few crossed wires, but people seemed to know more about you than you think. You know what someone told your poor father? 'Oh, we think he's off for the night and out with his floozy.' "

Programme of Events

Monday, September 29, 1947

7.00 a.m.—Swimming Pool and Gymnasium available
11.45 a.m.—Morning Music   Main Lounge
    Geraldo's Sextet, directed by Harry Hurst
4.00 p.m.—Music for Teatime   Main Lounge
    Geraldo's Sextet, directed by Harry Hurst
4.15 p.m.—Movie: "SONG OF THE SOUTH"
    Cinema
7.20 p.m.—News Broadcast   Main Lounge
9.00 p.m.—Orchestral Selections   Main Lounge
    Geraldo's Sextet, directed by Harry Hurst
9.30 p.m.—Movie: Repetition of above
    Programme   Cinema
9.45 p.m.—Horse Racing   Main Lounge
10.30 p.m.—Dancing   Ballroom
    Geraldo's Orchestra, directed by Harold Fields
11.15 p.m.—Auction Pool   Smoke Room
Midnight.—Dancing   Verandah Grill
    Geraldo's Orchestra, directed by Harold Fields

FC

ROTARIANS travelling by this ship are invited to inspect the Rotary Register at the Purser's Office and subscribe their names. The Purser will be glad, providing circumstances permit, to arrange an informal meeting during the voyage.

CLOCKS

Clocks will be advanced ten minutes every hour on the hour from 6—11 p.m.

CUNARD WHITE STAR LIMITED

FORM A 183 A—190A   L.P.15 467.

CUNARD WHITE STAR LIMITED

CREW LANDING CARD—U.S.A.

Date.... **24th September, 1947**

Ship.... **R.M.S. "QUEEN MARY"**

Name.... *Hurst H.*

Rating.... *Musician*

Sheet No.... *5*   Line No.... *22*

Harry opened his mouth to remonstrate but Rose was on a roll and pushed on. "Not to mention that ghastly scandal in India when you stripped off stark naked under the window of … who was it? … the wife of your commanding officer. Drunk and serenading her with your violin, so I heard. Yes, you think I didn't hear about all these things – word travels, you know."

Whatever love was left between them seemed to have evaporated on that night, when Rose confronted him so forcefully with just a few of his wrongdoings. Harry of course harboured a level of considerable guilt, knowing his wrongdoings were way more than Rose ever suspected. He began to feel he'd really made a mess of things. Rose had suggested in no uncertain terms that he head back to England and sort himself out. See if he even wanted to be with a wife and a lovely daughter, while she, in the meantime, would ponder if she really was up for having any further life with him.

Back in London, Harry recalled he had actually felt a sense of relief: no one to be answerable to, and a chance to reinvent his life. He got himself quite a bit of work playing violin on various shows at BBC Radio London.

And then one day, picking up *The Times,* he'd seen the article saying the *Queen Mary* would soon be sailing again between London and New York. The liner would have a resident dance band and they were looking for someone to be co-leader of that band with esteemed bandleader Geraldo.

Geraldo Bright had been around for decades, and was a very popular and successful conductor. He was now concentrating on getting bands onto those great trans-Atlantic liners, especially appealing for musicians from England and the USA. Both those countries had reciprocal bans on their artists from working in each other's countries. But now, getting on a liner and sailing the Atlantic was a great way to avoid those restrictions. When the liners docked in New York, musicians could have a couple of free nights to visit the iconic jazz clubs in Broadway, Manhattan and Greenwich Village.

Harry hadn't needed to think twice. He had submitted his application and was accepted. The liner, restored to her full glory, made her first trans-Atlantic trip on 31 July 1947, with Harry and his violin safely on board.

Now, with the afternoon sun shining on his face and a gentle breeze blowing off the sea, he felt an even greater sense of relief at being freed from his former life. Maybe it had all been for the best. What amorous adventures might this extravagant ship, with its destination city New York, have in store for him?

LOCAL MAN LEADS 'Q.M.' ORCHESTRA

Leader of the orchestra on the Queen Mary for the winter season is a Golders Green man, Mr. Harry Hurst, of Basing Hill.

He went to the Guildhall School of Music, where he studied the violin, conducting and composing. Then he joined the R.A.F. as an air-gunner, and saw over five years' service, during which time he was on several operational flights over Germany. He also served in India, and on several occasions played for the Viceroy at Vice-regal Lodge, and broadcast on the all-India radio.

MR. HARRY HURST

Invalided out of the Service, he went to Palestine, and regularly broadcast on the Palestine radio.

Since returning to England, he has been on the air with the B.B.C. Variety Orchestra, Vic Oliver, George Melachrino, Serge Krish and the New Metropolitan Orchestra, Geraldo, Rae Jenkins and Frank Cantell.

He has also broadcast several times with Peter Yorke.

Chapter 16
Life on the wicked stage

Richard Leacroft was a much-loved director of the repertory company. He and his wife Helen were proving to be invaluable in helping Grace settle into her new life. Helen took the young woman under her wing and helped her search for suitable lodgings, which everyone colloquially referred to as digs.

Few people earning their money from the theatre could afford to live solo, so Grace was teamed up with another actress in the company, Wendy Houghton. Wendy was a bubbly woman, buxom without being fat, with peroxided blonde hair, a broad smile and a warm rasping laugh.

The two women sat at the tiny kitchen table sharing a pot of tea and smoking Wild Woodbines.

"I hope I won't be a burden for you," Grace offered Wendy, an apologetic look on her face.

"Good God, no!" exclaimed Wendy. You'd have to be better than my last live-in companion. She got herself knocked up, you know, and just disappeared to God knows where."

Seeing the shock on Grace's face, Wendy laughed out loud.

"Oh you are a naïve young thing, aren't you? If you're wanting a life on the wicked stage, you need to get used to these sorts of things happening. Not like your usual life in a quiet street with roses in the front yard, you know!"

"I think I'll cope," offered Grace. "I'm just so excited to get this chance."

Wendy sat looking thoughtfully at Grace.

"You should do well if you've got the talent. You've certainly got the looks for it. You know, you look like an angel. I think you should give yourself a stage name – Angela. What do you think? I think it suits you perfectly."

And so, just like that, Grace, the child fair of face, became Angela, the woman with the angel's face!

The thrill of being part of a real theatre group was beyond anything Angela could have wished for. It was also endless hard work. A play was cast, the next week it was rehearsed, and while it was being performed on stage for barely a week, the next was being cast. Hence the name Repertory Group.

Angela's first role was in *The Second Mrs Tanqueray,* in which she played a very proper daughter trying to forge a bond with her new stepmother. Reviews of her performance were glowing. "Newcomer Angela Dent shines in her first role."

It was the first of many favourable reviews, as Angela's career went from strength to strength.

Chapter 17
Harry overplays his hand

The jazz clubs of New York were a magnet for Harry. They seemed to be a melting pot for a cross-section of New York society – the beautiful people flaunting their money, up-and-coming musicians plus those who already had made a name for themselves; and shady businessmen offering all sorts of post-war contraband for sale.

Silk stockings were especially popular among the men buying seductive gifts for their women. The heavy-set man in charge of selling the stockings moved among the customers as they sat drinking and listening to the music.

"Hey fella, wanna get some nylons for yer dame? Ya know, these gals are so wild over nylons, they'll do just about anythin' for yer after."

The idea of a "dame" doing just about anything in exchange for a pair of stockings was pretty appealing to Harry. He fossicked in his trouser pocket and pulled out a small roll of notes. A thought crossed his mind. These things were in short supply in London. Maybe if he bought a few, he could turn a small profit when he returned.

"I'll take six pairs, if you can spare them."

"Hey, you musta got a lot of dames there, fella," said the vendor with a lascivious grin.

~~~

One night Harry and his fellow orchestra member Reg, a trumpeter, were in a club where the races mixed freely and where coloured musicians were pioneering a new form of
~~~

jazz called bebop. It was considered quite shocking in those days, even in New York, to see coloured people dancing with white people.

The joint was literally jumping, the women in their flared frocks and bobby socks, twirling and turning, breasts bouncing, skin gleaming with perspiration. Many of the men sported dapper suits with colourful contrasting ties, and shiny shoes that literally slid across the floor as they gyrated to the beat.

Two women with honey-coloured skin and gleaming black hair slipped into the spare chairs at the table where Harry and Reg sat, ogling the dancers and revelling in the music.

"Hi guys. Where you all from? Wanna buy us a drink?"

"Well, sure thing!" Reg piped up enthusiastically.

Harry found himself mesmerised by Francesca, or at least that's the name the voluptuous black woman gave him. It didn't take more than one pair of those stockings to get her to invite him back to her tiny loft apartment, where he discovered the delights of a woman the Americans liked to call "hot to trot".

~~~

The trans-Atlantic liner had become Harry's new home. Each evening he dressed up, along with the other band members, in his black suit and bow tie, performing melodies to get people dancing. He felt like a bit of a celebrity, and was not-so-secretly delighted with the admiring glances many of the women threw his way.

There was a lot of wealth on board that ship. Wealthy Texas ranchers, wealthy New York stockbrokers, wealthy men of questionable background, and all of them sported glamorous women hanging off their arms, sometimes dripping in pearls
~~~

and diamonds and furs. Some of the men loved to gamble at night, setting up poker games which went until the early hours of the morning. Some disgruntled, neglected wives thought they'd seek out a bit of their own fun, and one night a petite blonde in a very low-cut dress cast her glance Harry's way.

During the band's break she sauntered over to him, asking flirtatiously if he would play her favourite song, "Slow Boat to China" in the next set. Harry and the band duly obliged, and at the end of that set she seductively beckoned him over to her table.

"I guess we're on a pretty good slow boat here, and my husband won't be back tonight. Too busy gambling, you know. Makes me feel so lonely. Could use some company. I'm Lena, by the way."

She looked at him from beneath fluttering false eyelashes, and Harry felt himself again being drawn into the siren call of a very attractive, very available woman.

And so, between Francesca when in port, and women like Lena when at sea, each journey was a smorgasbord of pleasure, and all the while he was earning a good living. Such a shame, then, that it would all soon come to a crashing halt.

~~~

As the *Queen Mary* docked, Harry tucked his precious violin under his arm and grabbed his suitcase which, during this trip, housed not only his dinner suit and music play sheet, but was also crammed with the precious silk stockings.

Moving towards customs, he fully expected to breeze through as he had done several times before.

A gruff looking man with a broad Lancashire accent barked, "Suitcase there please! Let's see what you've got."
~~~

There was nowhere to run or hide. Snapping the clasps and opening the lid, Harry felt panic rise up, as the customs officer's eyes widened.

"What 'ave we got here then?" he asked. "What are you doing with so many of these? Can't have that many wives and girlfriends, I'd wager."

Needless to say, those in charge of employing Harry were extremely embarrassed and angry to have such a high-profile member of their team caught out in what was basically a smuggling act. His contract was terminated with immediate effect. No more stolen hours with Francesca or women with names like Lena, Gladys and Mary-Lou. Back to boring old London, playing contracts on the radio, and maybe some restaurant work.

He knew for sure by now that there was no way he intended to return to Palestine, which was now Israel. Too much danger and conflict, and at heart he had no inclination to resume his marriage. Both he and Rose had moved on.

Chapter 18
Theatrical shenanigans

Angela's relatively sheltered life didn't prepare her for all the "goings-on", as Wendy called them, inherent in the group.

Love affairs seemed to be a dime a dozen, members of the group falling in and out of bed with each other like changing shoes.

"Oh Angela, you're so old-fashioned," Wendy berated her jokingly one night as they sat at their tiny dining table, quelling pre-show nerves with a small sherry. "I'd think maybe you've never even been with a man." She raised her eyebrows questioningly at Angela, who blushed, remembering that night back in the army with Chuck. It had put her off the whole idea of getting up close and personal with a man again.

"I think John might have a bit of a thing for you," joked Wendy.

John was one of the leading men in their company – handsome enough, but full of himself and obviously with a roving eye for as many ladies as he could ensnare.

"Oh, I really couldn't imagine it!" Angela blurted out, a look of distaste crossing her face. "He seems sort of arrogant. And he may be an actor but he has no culture! I'd prefer a more artistic, modest type." She paused to reflect. "Who do you fancy then, Wendy?"

Pretending to be coy, Wendy grinned and spread her hands in a confessional gesture. "Well, to tell the truth I was at a little restaurant a few weeks ago down in West London, and there was a fellow there – a sort of strolling violinist. Doing requests for the customers. A bit of a looker; got these lovely hands, if you get what I mean. I must say, we've spent a bit of time together and he's quite a ladies' man. Knows how to use those hands."

"Ooh, do tell more!" Angela cajoled with a slightly embarrassed giggle.

"I better not tell too much, you might fancy him."

The women laughed conspiratorially together then, glancing at the clock, realised they'd better hotfoot it down to the theatre for the night's performance.

~~~

Angela's career went from strength to strength. The reviews were always glowing, whether she was in a tiny role or something more substantial. But the schedule was gruelling, with three plays in various stages of production at once. It was a recipe for over-exhaustion and Angela often found herself barely able to drag one foot in front of the other. The Spartan condition of the inadequately heated lodgings didn't help either, and often one or other of the women fell ill with throat and chest infections.

She and Wendy shared their modest digs together amiably, but of late Wendy had seemed not her usual self, a little glum even. Angela had asked her what was wrong, but Wendy just shrugged it off.

One afternoon, in between rehearsal and the evening's performance, there was a loud rapping on the door. Angela opened it to find Beryl, their landlady, standing there with curlers in her hair and a cigarette drooping from her mouth.

In her rasping voice, Beryl called through the doorway, "Wendy – there's a geezer on the phone for ya. 'E says it's urgent."
~~~

Angela's Leicester Repertory publicity shot

Wendy retuned from the phone call looking unusually flustered, and Angela thought she even detected a black smudge below the eyes, indicating that her usually strong friend may have been crying.

"What is it? What's upset you so?" Angela solicitously put her hand over Wendy's.

"That bastard!" exclaimed Wendy. "He thinks he can run around with other women, then come crawling back to me. Well he can't." She burst into a fresh flood of tears.

The next day when Wendy was again summoned to the phone, she looked imploringly at Angela.

"Be a darling will you, Ange, just take the call and tell him to bugger off."

Angela followed Beryl down the gloomy corridor, noting her landlady's ragged pink slippers and defeated shuffle. At the same time she wondered what she would say to this "geezer" who had obviously broken Wendy's tough heart.

Picking up the phone she mustered her courage.

"Hello."

"Well, hello, that doesn't sound like Wendy." It was a well-spoken voice, neither high nor deep, and with just a hint of a Cockney accent.

"No, it's not. Wendy told me to tell you to bugger off," Angela blurted out, feeling triumphant and a little embarrassed.

There was a silence at the other end, then an amused chuckle.

"Well, can I at least know the name of the lovely lady who's telling me to bugger off?"

And so began a series of regular phone calls in which Harry tried, with increasingly less determination, to roust up Wendy, and Wendy sent Angela to the phone to deliver the usual message. The pair had fallen to chatting, almost like friends, with the matter of Wendy increasingly unimportant.

After a couple of weeks of this, Harry got a little braver.

"I'd love to meet you in person, Angela dear. I mean, how long can a fellow be abused by someone who sounds so adorable, and still not get to see her face? Perhaps we could meet up for a nice cuppa one afternoon."

Angela had to admit their regular chats had piqued her curiosity. Harry had told her about his musical career, they had shared stories of their respective wartime experiences, and there was something about the man that was intriguing, though she couldn't pinpoint just what.

"Oh, I don't think that's a good idea," she responded.

"Come on, dear, what have you got to lose? How about a nice cuppa and cake at Fortnum's whenever you're next down in London."

Oooh, thought Angela, the offer sounded too good to refuse so she reluctantly agreed.

Chapter 19
When Angela met Harry

She was overdue for a few days' rest, and unusually, not having a role in the latest production, Angela took the train down to London. Money was always tight, so she decided she should make the 45-minute walk from the station to Charing Cross where she and Harry had agreed to meet. It was cold, but she soon warmed up from the exertion, arriving out of breath, but exactly on time.

Oh, he's nothing like I imagined from his voice on the phone, thought Angela as she walked towards the man looking nervously around him, obviously waiting for someone. He wore a brown tweed overcoat, with a scarf wrapped around his neck and tan leather gloves. As she neared him, Angela was struck by the fineness of his features, long straight nose and bright blue eyes, that suddenly locked onto hers and seemed to light up.

"Angela?" he asked with an expectant raise of his eyebrows. His voice was just as she remembered it on the phone.

She felt suddenly awkward, and also a little flustered, as there was something about him that instantly appealed to her, though exactly what she didn't know.

"Ah yes, that's me. Harry, I presume?"

"Come," he said laughingly and gently placing his hand on the small of her back to guide her towards the store entrance. "Let's get out of this cold. We can chat over a nice cuppa."

They settled themselves in a corner table amid the hustle and bustle of the Clermont, a delightful old afternoon tea venue that was obviously doing a booming trade in scones and other indulgent treats.

Harry extricated himself from his overcoat and scarf, then carefully removed his gloves and placed them on the table. Angela was instantly struck by his hands: shapely, delicate, and what she thought of as artistic-looking. Surely a real musician's hands. She couldn't help but remember what Wendy had said about those hands.

"So you're in theatre, eh? A perfect career for such a delightful looking creature."

Angela wasn't sure she liked being called a creature, but there was something in the way he engaged her conversationally, held her eyes with his, and put her at ease so quickly. Any awkwardness or apprehension she'd felt soon melted away, as they fell effortlessly into conversation, and revelation, about their lives and their wartime experiences. Before she knew it, three hours had passed and it was time to head back to Leicester.

Angela arrived back at her digs via the last train. She found Wendy still up, sitting at the table, smoking and going over lines.

Wendy looked quizzically at Angela's flushed face. "So, how did you find him? You give him a good dressing down? He's a mongrel, that one!"

"I have to say, I found him quite charming," responded Angela, a slightly embarrassed smile on her face. "I think he liked me. In fact, he's coming up for a visit in a couple of weeks."

<center>~~~</center>

Exactly what took place over those early years between Harry and Angela, Sarah would never know. How their early dates

The early happy days of Angela and Harry

went, when they first fell into a sexual relationship, how often they saw each other. None of it had ever been alluded to, let alone talked about by Angela during all those wonderful mother-daughter bonding sessions on a Saturday night when Harry was out playing his fiddle.

The mystery was set in train when Sarah was a young girl, but the big revelation would come many years after that, when Sarah was in her mid-thirties.

Chapter 20

A childhood memory – those old letters

The joy of the lockdown being lifted hadn't lasted long. Before a few months had passed, the powers that be declared more restrictions should be placed upon the population, to curb the ongoing spread of Covid. Nothing for it but to once again attack the vault of her history lurking in the cupboards.

The clean-up had already taken on a life of its own. Attacking the cupboard in her office shelf by shelf, Sarah was constantly surprised at what she unearthed, the past long stuffed away in various states of order, disorder and total disarray.

Generally, she was an orderly person, and the many photos she'd gathered over the years were carefully displayed in albums, each one labelled with the year on its spine. But a few old random snaps had never quite made it to the filing system, and lurked in envelopes marked "to be filed".

"Ha, look at this!" she muttered to herself, as a dogeared old black and white picture slipped out of its moorings in an old greying envelope title "Random Snaps from my Childhood".

Eight-year-old Sarah and her parents stared into the camera. Who had taken this picture, she wondered.

Her smile looked happy and relaxed, those of her parents more forced. She was an only child and felt protected and much loved, so whatever issues were between her parents didn't seem to make her feel any less loved.

The trio in the photo were standing in front of the old fibro-cement garage, a place in which she had loved to play. The main attraction in the garage was the old steamer trunk, with its big brass locks and scratched blue exterior. It had travelled halfway across the world, accompanying her parents on the steamer to Australia. All manner of treasures and secrets lurked inside. One of her favourites was her father's old RAF bomber jacket, with its fur collar and creased leather.

One memorable afternoon, as she'd been trawling, yet again, through the magical trunk and its contents, she chanced upon a small rear pocket she hadn't seen before. Fossicking inside she extracted a small wad of yellowing envelopes, and recognised her mother's familiar, elegant writing on the outside. At that very moment her mother appeared **at** the side door of the garage.

The look of horror on Angela's face shocked Sarah, as the woman swooped and snatched the letters from Sarah's hands with an angry admonishment.

"Don't touch those — they're not yours."

Unaccustomed to being shouted at by her usually loving mother, Sarah burst into tears. Later at dinner she ventured to ask about the letters and why her mother had been so angry.

"Don't worry my love, just some old nonsense that should have been thrown out years ago," Angela replied. "Sorry to have yelled at you."

How easily her mother had dismissed those letters as old nonsense.

The letters had remained as good as vanished for nearly three decades.

Chapter 21
Secrets of the childhood trunk

After her divorce from Richy, Sarah had lived alone, albeit it with a steady stream of short-term and long-term lovers. Her modest cream brick veneer house brought her endless joy, whether it was pottering in her garden, pursuing DIY renovations, or entertaining friends with overindulgent dinner parties.

There was a garage too, mainly a storage spot for her garden tools. In the corner of the garage the old trunk from her childhood had come to reside, brought there by Harry when he and Angela had finally ended their marriage and he'd left their family home. The appeal of the trunk had long since evaporated, and she'd never even bothered to fossick into it.

"Hello, my darling!" Harry bellowed through the phone. "Can your old papa come on over for a cuppa and look into that trunk you've been minding for me? I need to find some old RAF papers that might help me get a British pension."

The trunk; she'd barely given it a thought in years.

"Of course, see you at three?"

Harry adored Sarah; she was his pride and joy, had been all her life, as far as she could remember, despite all the unhappiness within the home, and despite his so often not being there of an evening. She could see the delight on his face whenever he joined her for however short a catch up. This afternoon was no different, and after they'd sat for an hour or so, companionably sipping coffee and eating sticky bun, they headed into the garage.

The trunk was dusty with spider webs. Sarah brushed it off

with an old towel and watched as Harry opened the lid and began to rifle through the contents.

"Find what you're needing?" she casually asked.

Her father seemed to have become a little agitated. Among the old official-looking envelopes were a number of blue aerogram letters. Harry anxiously unfolded one, then another, his eyes scanning the contents, his teeth nervously nibbling at his lower lip.

Sarah went to stand behind him, trying to peer over his shoulder as he tried to angle the letters away from her. She had seen that the envelope was postmarked from Israel, and a couple of words on the actual letter caught her immediate attention: "... *Harry, our divorce ...*"

Abruptly Harry refolded the old blue letter, stacked it in a mound with another pile of papers, hefted the lot into his arms and headed towards his car, parked in Sarah's driveway.

"Lovely afternoon, darling, lovely. Have to get going now," he muttered, opening the car boot and unceremoniously dumping the bundle of papers in.

Sensing something amiss, Sarah put her hand on his arm. "Hang on there a minute, Dad – what's with all the secrecy? I saw something – something about a divorce." Her mind was clicking over at a rate of knots. "You weren't married before Mum, were you?"

Harry's face looked stricken. Good liar that he was, he couldn't give his daughter such a barefaced lie.

"Um, yes, I was. Not for long, though."

"Oh!" Sarah looked momentarily stunned. "But you never had any kids with her?"

The silence seemed interminable. In a barely audible voice Harry said, "Only one daughter."

Only one daughter! She, Sarah, was his one daughter! Why had she never been told this? A memory of that day so long ago suddenly came back to her, the day when she'd found old letters in the trunk in the garage, and her mother had angrily whisked them away. But how could these be the same letters? How had they found their way back into the trunk? How the hell could something so important have been kept from her?

She barked that very question at her father. His troubled face crumpled and, to her shock, he began to cry. She'd only ever seen him cry once before, the day before she had married Richy, when their beloved dog had been hit by a car and Harry had furiously dug a hole in the backyard to bury the adored pet.

"Darling, I never wanted you to find out, because I thought you wouldn't love your old Papa anymore."

And for the time being that was the only explanation she got, but it served to pacify her. In her general state of shock, she didn't think to stop Harry getting away with the letters, which were not to surface again until after his death several years later.

Chapter 22
RIP Harry

Sarah remembered all too clearly the night her father died. It was soon after she'd met David and she'd been staying over at his place. They were anticipating an early night together so she was already in her pyjamas.

Harry had been in hospital for several days following an unexpected heart attack. A couple of weeks earlier, a young incompetent doctor had diagnosed his chest pains as indigestion and sent him home with antacid tablets. But the pains hadn't gone away, and then the big one had hit, and now, recovering in hospital, Harry was due to come home.

In fact, Sarah and David had visited him just the day before, and he'd asked if they could bring him a gun, as he wanted to shoot the television sets in his ward, so much did the noise of them aggravate him! Sarah had planned to collect him in a couple of days, but then came the unexpected, shocking phone call.

She'd dressed and headed to the hospital where she sat for a while with his body, berating him out loud for having gone and died. No matter what his failings, and how aggravating and childish he could be at times (not to mention the angst he had caused her mother), Sarah had loved him dearly.

It was almost unbelievable. This active and vibrant man, always full of life and entertaining others, had succumbed too young. He was only seventy-nine. She'd thought he'd go on for many more years. Apart from the occasional attack of back pain, he seldom seemed to be in ill health, at least as far as Sarah knew..

Perhaps all those years of playing his violin in smoke-filled restaurants, before the ban on cigarettes, had contributed to his weak heart. She remembered how vehemently he had loathed smoking.

The usually animated Harry now lay still and grey, and Sarah sat in shock, tears streaming down her face. Gradually she ceased her sobbing, kissed her father's forehead, then took out her Swiss army knife and cut off a lock of his hair. It would stay in her jewellery box to this day.

The next couple of days were taken up with organising a funeral and, unsure of what he wanted, Sarah paid a small tribute to his Jewish background by draping his prayer shawl over the coffin, but basically he was given a secular funeral, with tribute speeches and, of course, listening to recordings of his music.

~~~

Soon after Harry's death, a clean-up of another sort had begun.

Sarah remembered letting herself into the tiny bed-sit Harry had occupied since the days after he finally ended the marriage with Angela. Perhaps some would have seen it as squalid; she saw it as poignant, sad and downright depressing.

Flinging open the cupboard that was supposedly for storage of linen, she was aghast at the clutter and jumble of things accumulated there.

Out tumbled two pairs of shabby shoes, followed by two spare violin bows, the horse hair already broken loose from its moorings. A desiccated sandwich lurked in the corner, with a pair of pyjama bottoms carelessly tossed on top. Newspaper cuttings seemed to fill the spaces, along with single socks and the odd pair of shabby y-fronts.
~~~

How could anyone live like this, she wondered.

And then suddenly there they were, unexpectedly neat, bundled up with an elastic band keeping them together – letters and more letters. It was tempting to read them then and there, but there was serious work to be done. She began to sort out bundles of things – those to go to trash, those to send to the opportunity shop, and those, like the letters, that would be taken home with her, to examine more carefully another day.

Chapter 23
The fateful letters re-emerge

Another day had in fact taken almost thirty years. Sure, she had scanned them cursorily the day she'd discovered them, but, for whatever reason, had filed them away in her memorabilia box.

Now, during the lockdown, with all the time in the world, she could examine her parents' past at her leisure. Carefully pulling out the bundle of letters, she began to randomly read, then decided better of it. Why not put them in some sort of chronological order, like a series of markers to the dark corners of Harry's life she hadn't really known.

With a gasp she recognised Angela's handwriting on a pair of ivory-coloured envelopes, sporting stamps of King George V in the corner, and postmarked 1949. More recent letters, still in envelopes, had postmarks dating them back to the 1970s. These she put to one side and carefully set the older letters out on the kitchen table.

It was those letters, the ones her mother had been so upset about and had then whisked away from her, told her so much.

It seems that early in 1949, when Harry and Angela had been dating for some time, Angela was diagnosed with tuberculosis and was forced to spend time isolated in a sanitorium. The wretched digs in which she and Wendy had lived, combined with a rigorous work schedule, a poor diet and the English cold, had certainly done her no favours.

The antibiotic streptomycin had been developed in 1944, and fortunately it, along with rest and time spent in the fresh air, had helped cure her of the potentially fatal disease.

As the time neared for her release she had written to Harry:

May 1949: Good news depending on the results of my last test ... I can't possibly be positive ... of course should we leave the country I can always go elsewhere for a checkup ... I love you so much and am so anxious to be with you. Your Angela.

Leave the country? Obviously they must have holidayed overseas from England.

Sarah also had the old photo albums her mother had given her when she and Harry had divorced. She'd never been especially interested in them until now, but she eagerly pulled one off the shelf. The lovely fluted edges of the old black and whites confirmed that, in their early courting days, Angela and Harry had indeed spent many a happy time together on holiday, on occasion at Tintagel in Cornwall, another time in Switzerland, in the bucolic village of Kandersteg. Sarah continued to read eagerly, opening each letter with a fluttering heart and sense of anticipation.

June 1949: Beloved ... am delighted that you will be here on Friday. I'm neither unhappy nor lonely, but your arrival will make everything so complete and beautiful ... I love you so much dearest and so look forward to being with you again. Your adoring Angela.

No date: I am feeling 150% now, and am waiting for the extra 50% when you arrive to be with me once again.

And another: I'll be out for your birthday without a doubt, your loving, lecherous Angela.

Lecherous! Sarah was astonished to see that her mother had once felt that way about her father. All she had ever seen was vitriol, contempt and distress. Not to mention the single beds all their married life, followed by separate rooms for the last couple of decades of their time together. Hah! No wonder Angela had been at such pains to see that Sarah never found those letters. For some reason, she never wanted Sarah to know how much she had loved the man she ended up seemingly despising.

More letters confirmed that the love affair had stayed strong for at least another year.

December 1949: … It's funny how with the progress of time one finds it increasingly difficult to express words of affection towards a loved one. Not because one cares less; I care more, so much more … our feelings are so intense as to defy expression. I look back on these past two years with such gratitude, you have afforded me so much happiness. I never thought to be so happy for so long. I think of all the little things we have done and seen together, even our upsets and worries, and they all merge into one big whole, one big feeling of love and desire for you. I shall always feel like this, I have no doubt of it. All my love always, Angela.

1950: To my very own Harry, In love and gratitude for the three happiest years I have ever known, and for the knowledge that no matter what comes, we shall always be happy.

Sarah surprised herself by slumping to the floor and dissolving into a flood of tears. How could this be? How was it possible that there once had been such intense love and passion between her parents, the same two she remembered as having virtually hated each other for so long. The parents whose lives had been such a model of bitterness, anxiety and aggression had once been totally in love. Angela had actually been besotted with Harry. How could such love and lust have turned into such animosity?

This called for a calming glass of wine, or two, which she polished off while rereading the letters.

Okay, she finally thought, I guess most broken marriages started off with love. Of course I know that only too well; look at me and Richy. And perhaps it's nice to know that, with all the ugly scenes, and sniping and what looked like hatred, there had in fact once been love and passion between her parents.

That wasn't quite the end of the early letters though. Undated, but some time later, came this heartbreaker from Angela:

Firstly I ask myself what it is that attracted me to you and I believe the answer is that in you I see the personification of an ideal or imagined I did. What do I want of you? To be with you. But I know what I don't want and that is to become just another affair, a person you met, liked and slept with then discarded. I should hate that and should further hate you for using me so. Why should I hate it? Because I love being with you. None of the silly doubts, fears and suspicions assail as they do with the other men I know and have known. Above all, this, I feel, is a relationship that must be safeguarded since it is a rare and wonderful relationship, one that I have rarely, if ever, experienced. It is a relationship upon which all my hopes, dreams, even fears have been hinged on; a relationship I hoped existed but hardly dared believe did. Now that at last I find that it does exist, I must do nothing to force me to renounce my claim to the pleasure you afford me, nothing that will cause this realised ideal to slip from my grasp to be recaptured only in futile dreams. I say recaptured only in dreams since I shouldn't have sufficient fight to look for it again in material form. Whatever I have achieved in this life, I have fought for. And whereas I must forcibly go on fighting since it is my destiny, I can only fight for the preservation of the things I have. I cannot struggle again toward the goal that came into view and then disappeared like a mirage because of some stupid lack of foresight on my part.

That train of thought being in a morbid vein, my subsequent thoughts were morbid. I asked myself what right I had to think that my feelings were reciprocated, that obviously you regarded me in no other way than the rest, that any highfalutin ideas you cherished could not find realisation in me and so I might just as well become reconciled to the fact and treat you as I might treat any other men of my acquaintance. Yet whilst I told myself this, I could see your face floating above wearing the sad expression I saw twice on Monday ...

The rest of this letter was almost illegible, its blue ink having faded over more than sixty years. What content was decipherable seemed to fade away in vague waffling.

Something else about this last letter deeply disturbed Sarah. Could her mother's penchant for over-analysing and self-reflection be almost an inherited trait? Many of Sarah's own writings so recently unearthed carried similar self-indulgent ramblings with overtones of 'analysis paralysis'.

In terms of seeing the inexorable decline in her parents' relationship, this last letter showed enough for Sarah to see the writing on the wall. Obviously Angela was starting to feel she could possibly be just one of many to her beloved Harry. To think that her mother had felt so intensely about love, and had felt such an obsessive fear of rejection! She who had seemed to Sarah as a child so strong, and yet so vulnerable; she who never wanted to show she cared for Harry.

The rest Sarah knew from what her mother had told her over the years. Angela had finally had enough of Harry and his wandering ways; she summoned up the courage to make a break and head overseas. She applied to Canada but they didn't want her because of her tubercular history. And so the relocation to the great land Down Under was planned. She would break loose from her grand love affair with Harry and start over. But in the tradition of that wonderful song "If you leave me, can I come too?", Harry decided he couldn't let such a good woman go, promised to be more the man she had idealised him as, and followed her to Australia.

They bought a ten-pound ticket on a steamer called the *Strath Naver*. The men and women were separated, and Angela shared an overcrowded cabin with several other women, one of whom had a baby and festooned every spare inch with drying nappies.

The old photo album, the same one with the pictures of Switzerland, showed their boat crossing the equator, with much fun and frivolity had by all. And after several weeks of challenging sailing, a far cry from the luxury cruises of today, their ship landed them in Melbourne, with all their worldly goods packed into the famous steamer trunk that so fascinated Sarah when she was a child, and which contained the revelatory letters.

How much emotional upheaval could a person stand in one day? Tired out with the reading and the revelations, not to mention the several glasses of wine, Sarah slumped into bed. She slept fitfully, dreaming of her childhood, the trunk, her parents, and some man from her own past who had cheated on her; just who it was she couldn't get a grasp on when she awoke, exhausted from so many disturbing dreams.

~~~

Despite her troubled sleep, her impatience saw her up early the next morning, shuffling once again through the pile of letters. Those she had read, with English stamps and postmarks, she carefully laid to one side. Proof, precious proof of a love never seen by her, and never acknowledged by her mother.

A batch of familiar-looking blue aerograms caught her eye next. Surely they must be those she had seen Harry extract from the trunk that fateful day when he had been at pains to hide his past from her, the day she found out about his first marriage and his other daughter.

Sarah saw that these letters were postmarked Palestine. They must be from Harry's first wife, Rose. It was too early for wine, so maybe a second coffee while she read through this batch.
~~~

Here were the Israel postmarked letters again. She opened the first which had a date handwritten at the top – 1957. It was signed by Rose, and it was the letter in which Sarah had glimpsed those words "your divorce". Reading on, she saw that Rose had obviously been hounding Harry for a divorce, and Harry had been stalling, for whatever reasons. He had also been saying how his life with Angela and his beloved daughter Sarah could be quite destroyed if this news got out.

Like a bolt of lightning, things suddenly became clear. The dates of Harry's divorce from Rose and his marriage to Angela did not tally. Sarah's devious old dad had been a bigamist! He had married Angela when his marriage to Rose had not been officially terminated. A letter dated two years later showed that, to everyone's relief, finally legal proceedings had been concluded, but only after Rose had graciously said she would never tell a soul, as long as Harry granted her a divorce.

But that was only one part of the puzzle. Again Sarah pondered how such intense love could so easily turn to loathing. Her mother's carefully constructed persona was possibly a result of the extreme disappointment she had felt in Harry, as his behaviour reverted to the philanderer he had so often been. At least this was Sarah's assumption, based on the endless flirtatious style she had witnessed in her father all her young life. Combined with the tricky situation of Harry still having marital ties to Rose in Israel, it certainly was not a good start or ongoing basis for a solid marriage.

Chapter 24

Angela and Harry start afresh Down Under

Sometimes it was hard to remember what were actual memories, as opposed to what was implanted in her brain by her parents' stories. Perhaps what she imagined were memories were just recollections of photos she had seen. Angela had always liked to take photographs, and had carefully mounted many shots of their early lives in albums with transparent leaves separating each page. And here they were – the old photo albums, a repository of memories of what Sarah remembered as a happy childhood.

Harry and Angela had started their life in Australia renting a modest flat in the Melbourne suburb of Kew, and Harry soon got work by day as a clerk, along with several evenings a week playing his violin.

Harry, Angela and baby Sarah

Angela soon discovered she was pregnant with Sarah, and they had a hasty registry office wedding, and then decided to buy their own house. And what a dreary L-shaped weatherboard house it looked to be, from those tiny old black and white photos. An empty backyard with a Hills hoist, a far cry from the lush garden she remembered her mother later creating with love and backbreaking toil. In several

An almost happy family?

shots, the proud parents stood on the back step cradling a tiny baby in their arms, the small promise of hope radiating from their faces.

As baby Sarah grew, she seemed, from the photos, to be a cheery and chubby little soul, frolicking in the yard under the hose, feeding the chickens down in the coop, and later making sand castles on the beach during the family holidays to the seaside township of Rye. There were even a few photos of Angela's half-sister, Sheila. Sarah remembered Angela

telling her the two had eventually made a closer connection, and subsequently Angela had sponsored Sheila to come to Australia.

At the back of one photo album was a large manila envelope, and upon opening it up Sarah discovered aging newspaper clippings and yet more photos, all devoted to Harry and the many and varied places he'd graced with his violin playing.

In the early days of the marriage, one of the local radio stations, 3UZ, had run a weekly competition in which local hopefuls entered to test their talents. It was called *Are you an Artist?* Harry, along with his piano accordion accompanist, known to Sarah as Uncle Jack, often won.

Reviews were very favourable.

"Harry showed imagination and showmanship".

"Temperament, not temper, showed on the scowling face of violinist Harry, who is said to be one of the most likeable artists on the program."

All lovely stuff for feeding an artist's ego, and Harry had obviously kept as much of this ego-boosting memorabilia as he could.

Sarah found herself lingering over wonderful old 8x10 black and white studio photos, as Harry and various random women, probably other competitors, posed for the photographer, clustered around the incredibly large microphones that were part of broadcasting studios in those days. Many of the photos had been used in a weekly newspaper called the *Listener In,* an indispensable TV and radio guide.

But even more memorable was the locally run talent quest, *Swallows Parade,* that aired regularly on the television, an amazing new adjunct to suburban lives. You had to look your best for the new-fangled phenomenon, even if it was in black and white. The trouble was that Angela and Harry did not have much disposable money, so they had neither a TV set

Harry serenades Hollywood starlet Ann Miller at Mario's restaurant

nor money for fancy costumes. So Angela set about creating a special outfit for Harry. It was a waistcoat that had no buttons, as it was made of green plastic. Ever creative, Angela had collected umpteen silver milk bottle tops, squashed them flat, and sewn them on like sequins. Somehow, the pair pulled it off, and, given the TVs of the day were tiny and lacking in clarity, all the sparkle made Harry look like a real star.

Sarah remembered well the neighbours clustering together at the home of another neighbour up the street who was fortunate enough to have a TV set. They were all there to watch Harry, and she remembered feeling an element of pride.

Interspersed among the TV and radio publicity shots were several others of Harry, wielding his violin and serenading beautiful women in fancy restaurants. Melbourne was just starting to blossom with a few European-styled clubs and restaurants – Troika and Mario's being popular with the glamorous set, and the management loved having a cosmopolitan strolling violinist like Harry.

Album cover for one of the records made as
part of the Leo Rosner Band

In the photos where he was playing for women, he often seemed to be somehow wooing them or staring down their low-necked dresses, while they looked on adoringly at him.

That violin! Maybe it was Harry's secret weapon, making women fall hook, line and sinker for him. Sarah remembered how, as a child, when he had come towards her playing the fiddle, she had shrunk back in embarrassment. But most other listeners looked on in rapt attention, especially the women as he serenaded them, making them feel so special, making them feel for a brief moment perhaps they had been transported to Paris.

When he wasn't seducing women with his bowing technique, Harry did many gigs with notable Melbourne musicians, chief among them the renowned Leo Rosner band who played at Melbourne's most prestigious weddings, and barmitzvahs. Together the band released a couple of recordings at the Melbourne W&G studios. These 10-inch vinyl recordings were fondly remembered for a lifetime by those older

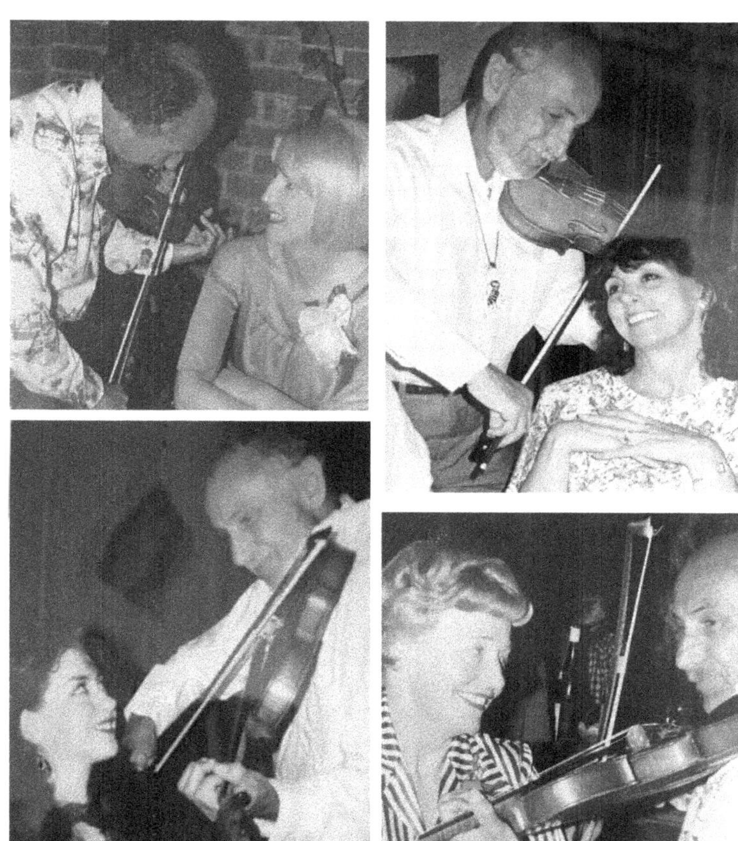

Harry's technique struck a chord with adoring women at The
Olive Tree, a restaurant where he played for many years

members of the Jewish community who danced to the music
at countless functions.

These functions seemed to be Harry's only remaining ties
with his Jewish upbringing. After marrying Angela he took on
the trappings of her Christian heritage, embracing Christmas
and Easter with gusto. His repertoire of carols on the violin
was vast, and he attacked Easter eggs enthusiastically, loving
to carefully straighten out their multi-coloured foil wrappers.

Chapter 25
Family life becomes more fraught

Hours flew by like minutes as Sarah allowed herself to become lost in the photos that took her back into her childhood, and the life the little trio shared. Sadly, it was a progressively detached trio, with the major familial bond being between Sarah and her mother, as Harry's musical life took precedence over everything else, and their marriage slowly became more and more embittered and hostile.

On Sunday afternoons, she remembered, Harry would spend hours in his armchair, eyes closed, Rachmaninoff or Mahler mournfully blaring from the stereo, as he listened intently, lost in thought, and nervously pulled stray hairs from his now greying moustache. If Angela or Sarah dared interrupt him, he'd shoo them off with a wave of his hand and an inarticulate grunt.

A sudden flash came to her of Angela and Harry arguing late one night. They had been out – a rare outing together, and a babysitter had looked after Sarah. They probably thought the child was asleep but through the half-open door Sarah could hear her mother's accusatory voice.

"How could you have made me feel so small and embarrassed me like that!"

Harry's placatory voice tried to soothe her. "I was only playing the song Lucy asked for."

"Playing! More like molesting her bosom with your violin bow. My God, I should never have given in and let you come with me to this godforsaken country!"

Their voices faded into the distance, with a few slamming doors, and from the far reaches of the house came the sounds of her mother's quiet sobbing.

Another memory flashed up of yet another acrimonious argument between her parents. What it was about, for the life of her she couldn't remember. All she could recall was her mother suddenly flinging a cup of hot tea at Harry. Fortunately, it missed the target, and the cup shattered against the door, leaving tea trickling down the now-chipped wood, and Harry standing like a stunned mullet, mouth agape, wondering what had just happened. Sarah also remembered that for some unknown reason she had found the whole performance somewhat funny.

The fact that Angela confided so much in her was also anything but amusing. Though heading for her teenage years, she was still relatively young after all, and didn't need to be told confidences about what the psychiatrist had said, what tranquilisers her parents were taking, and what deep and meaningful inner turmoil her mother was going through. Nor did she need to know that, as their sex life became less frequent, Harry would often leave some money under Angela's pillow, making her feel cheap and bought.

Harry had certainly held a tight monetary grip on the little family. Each week, when he'd brought home his pay, he and Angela had extracted several cigarette tins from the cupboard. They were labelled Gas, Electricity, Food, Other Expenses, and a set amount was carefully allotted to each tin. Angela had always felt she had to scrimp and save, and yet as years went past, Harry magically found money to make the occasional trip overseas.

Angela treated her daughter more like a friend and confidante than a child, and while Sarah adored the closeness, it made her feel, there was always a level of discomfort. To be so much the focus of someone else's life, their *raison d'etre;* it was daunting, even though at that young age she couldn't have articulated it. Those chickens would only come home to roost years later.

The unusually close mother-daughter bond did make for some fun Saturday nights, though. With Harry regularly out playing violin, Sarah and Angela would sit at the kitchen table and start up silly dialogues, spouting out nonsense lines in different accents. They especially loved speaking as if from the Bronx in New York. They talked loud and long about the fictional Auntie Doris, and Sarah found that once she started, she couldn't stop holding forth in silly voices.

Her mother was masterful with accents. She proudly boasted she could "do" any English regional brogue there ever was. She never mastered an Aussie accent, though!

This train of thought led Sarah to thinking back to Angela's creative life. Where was that scrapbook she knew her mother had so carefully and proudly compiled? More fossicking and hauling around of boxes produced a red-covered, scruffy but large scrapbook entitled *Life Upon the Wicked Stage.*

The opening pages featured carefully cut-out and pasted-in snippets of theatre reviews from her time in the English repertory companies. Like Harry's newspaper clippings, Angela's also had her name often underlined, with reviews variously describing her as versatile, consummate, employing rich comedy, delightfully cast and vivacious.

It was the early photos that enthralled Sarah, the young girl her mother had been before life beat her down, that angelic face, and the many gorgeous costumes that complemented her softly rounded body. Definitely like someone out of the movies, Sarah thought, feeling a deep pang of missing.

No wonder Harry was smitten with her upon their first meeting.

Because of Harry, her career had stalled once they came to Australia and she became a mother. She worked in several local theatre groups around Melbourne and established an enviable reputation, but it was not possible for two people to pursue night-time careers with a child to raise. Often Angela had dragged Sarah along to rehearsals, even after-show parties, so the young child had an eye-opening education highlighting the nature of these amateur theatre groups, with battling egos, flamboyant personalities and plenty of back-stabbing.

By the time she hit her teenage years, her parents' lives were even more estranged.

Sarah used to ask her mother, "Why on earth don't you two split up?"

"You know, the weak hold a terrible power over the strong," her mother told her. "He would just fall apart without me."

Or the other answer: "Because of you, my girl. You always said you didn't know which one of us you would live with and I couldn't take the risk of losing you."

What a burden that answer created for Sarah, as if she was somehow responsible for her mother's deep unhappiness.

The dysfunctional family life had drifted on for another eight or so years, in which Sarah excelled at school and was the focus of her parents' love, especially Angela's – the love her parents had lost for each other was all channelled into her.

Angela had kept a firm hold on her, in so many ways.

"I really want to learn the piano," Sarah had announced.

"No, that can't happen; we can't have you learning any instrument your father knows how to play; he'll be overbearing!"

And so Sarah had been given a guitar as compensation.

Then there was the opportunity when she was fourteen to apply for **an** exchange scholarship to Germany. Sarah was top of her class in the language, and would have been a shoe-in to get the trip.

"It's too dangerous, you're too young," she'd been told. Such a missed opportunity. More likely, Angela couldn't stand the thought of her precious daughter being away for so long. She'd be left to face the music with Harry all alone.

Even shopping for a dress for the first school social had brought control and conflict.

Harry and Angela still hanging in there

"I love this one with the sweetheart neckline!" Sarah had enthusiastically pulled a black dress off the rack and held it up against herself.

"That is not suitable, the neckline is too low," her mother had retorted. And so she'd gone off to the dance in a ghastly hot pink number with horrific bell sleeves and a high rounded neckline, piped with silver thread.

It was no wonder she had been so keen to marry Richy **to** get out of home, respectably, of course, as Angela would never have condoned her leaving just for the sake of being independent. As it was, Angela suffered when Sarah married, always seeming somehow resentful of Richy's easy-going family, which Sarah so obviously enjoyed being with. She visited her own parents less and less.

Chapter 26
When Sarah met David

Stuffed to the back of the cupboard was a box full of yet more cards. When she started trawling through them, Sarah realised with a start that these were, in fact, every card she and David had given each other during their 27-year relationship.

The first was a Valentine's card from the first year they had met.

"You're the gal for me – think I'm falling in love," it read in David's almost illegible scrawl.

Falling in love. Sarah pondered this expression long and hard. For David, that seemed to mean falling in lust – he was a man who was driven by sexual impulse, and had seemingly boundless energy for the activity.

Sarah's mind flitted back to their first meeting. A mutual friend, Sophie, had organised a dinner party, informing her that David would be perfect – just her type, in fact – Mediterranean-looking, with dark curly hair, dark eyes, neither fat nor thin, and sharing her passion for theatre.

~~~

Sophie ushered Sarah in as she handed over a bottle of medium-priced Shiraz. "Sarah, this is David," said Sophie, smugly already assuming she'd made a great match.

Well, he sure looks cute, thought Sarah, nodding and smiling at the appealing-looking fellow stuffing a handful of potato crisps into his mouth, then licking the salt from each finger.
~~~

"Oops, sorry." said David, wiping his hands on his jeans before shaking Sarah's outstretched hand.

Sarah was then introduced to another couple, who she thought she may have met before at Sophie's. At least there would be others to deflect the obviousness of Sophie's matchmaking attempt.

The dinner passed with engaged chatter, somewhat dominated by David, who was very keen to tell the gathering all about his recent promotion at work. He was an account manager with a large advertising company and, from how he told it, he was able to sell up a storm with alarming regularity. Hence he'd been promoted to handle the account for one of the city's burgeoning computer chains.

David had also recently divorced his wife of ten years; she'd shipped out with their son to Queensland, and he now had much more time to pursue his weekend and evening leisure activities, which consisted of playing in the local pool team, and having regular rounds of golf. Although he was obviously highly successful at his work, he seemed at greater pains to stress his success at sporting ventures, along with involvement in the creative arts He told everyone with pride that he was now on his fifth play script, although none had as yet been picked up by any theatre company.

"Oh, so you like theatre?" asked Sarah. "Seen the latest MTC production?"

"Oh no, I don't actually go to much; I prefer to create," was David's reply.

Sarah was a little bemused.

"Hmm, how can you create writing, when you don't put yourself out there absorbing what others do?" she asked.

"Well, that's their journey," responded David. "I follow my own journey – that's more important to me."

Ah, a man keen to be his own person, thought Sarah. I like that. Although, she still felt an edge of scepticism – how could he ever be a great writer, as he obviously wanted to be, if he didn't follow what other creative souls were doing?

The dinner guests lingered late in what was, all in all, an amiable and fun night. Sarah said her goodbyes, including to David, but when she reached her car, she was surprised to find him hovering near her.

"Sorry, didn't mean to startle you, just was hoping we could exchange numbers and maybe catch a movie some time," he suggested confidently.

Nothing ventured, nothing gained, thought Sarah, as she smiled and nodded.

"Sounds like a plan!" said David cheerily. It was one of his many lines she found fun at first, but then grew to recognise as part of a set repertoire of things to say, especially when he didn't want to reveal anything more deep or meaningful.

And so, almost fifteen years since her divorce from Richy, she began dating the man who would eventually become her second husband. Sarah soon came to see that behind his public persona, David was in fact a truly kind man, and perhaps it was his insecurities that made him talk up his achievements.

Although his ex-wife had taken the child, David wanted no more, probably never having wanted children in the first place. So that was one door which finally closed for Sarah. In many ways, it had probably been for the best, as she and David got to travel a lot, party a lot, and each could pursue their own activities at leisure.

<div align="center">~~~</div>

Yes, David's working life had certainly been a major success. Even though he had given up full-time work some time ago, he still freelanced as a consultant. To his astonishment and delight, a high-profile company for which he was doing a campaign over the internet decided they wanted to meet him in person, to nut out the details of the campaign together.

As luck (or bad luck) would have it, the flight left on March 10, 2020, when he flew to London. And on March 16, the first Covid lockdown in Victoria was declared.

Chapter 27
Life between marriages:
several sad and sorry affairs

The third Covid lockdown seemed to be dragging on forever. Sarah was champing at the bit for something to change, but she, like everyone else, could do nothing to hurry things along. The virus would take its time and the government obviously had no intentions of letting people off the leash. Oh well, nothing for it but to continue trawling through those boxes. Except these latest boxes were not so removed from her life as those containing her parents' past.

As she wrestled yet another ragged carton, dragging it down from the top shelf, it tipped over, spilling its contents over the hallway alcove. A blue aerogram fluttered down last from the upended box, as if to say "Read me first. I was the most important one of the many between your marriages." The letter was addressed to Sarah, but care of Roula, her old pal, who back then was living and working in Athens and residing in a cramped flat. Yes, Sarah had done another runner, yet again to Greece.

On the rear of the envelope was only a heart, and the name Robert scrawled next to it. In the letter he addressed her as "his beloved koala" (good God, was she that furry!?), and bemoaned the fact that he'd let the best thing in his life get away. With a jolt Sarah realised it wasn't that dissimilar to when Harry had chased Angela from England to Australia, fearful of losing his "best thing".

Sarah was the one who had felt finally she had to get away – escape from years of high drama at the hands of that letter-writer. Just the sight of Robert's name on that envelope accelerated her heartrate. What a time in her life that had been! What a crazy whirlwind of love, lust, deceit and betrayal.

~~~

After her marriage to Richy ended, Sarah had ridden the rollercoaster of love, loss and regret, and had definitely played the field. After the relationship with Jake had fizzled out, she embarked upon a series of one- or two-month stands, each time falling heavily for someone who didn't reciprocate her feelings, yet all the time hoping he might be "the one". Finally, when all that failed, she decided it would be a good idea to give it another go with Richy, but after he'd waited so long for her, while she ummed and aahed over what to do with her life, he had finally moved on and met another woman.

"Maybe we could try again Richy," she'd tentatively suggested.

"I'm sorry, Sarah, I've met someone and I think I will probably marry her." Richy was gentle but firm, and she couldn't help but feel with a sinking heart that she may have made the biggest mistake of her life. Maybe she'd let the best thing in her life go. What a fool I am, she mused. Married my first love too young, too young to really settle down, but too stupid to recognise how right for me he could have been.

At least her decisions about work had been sound ones. She'd long left teaching and embarked upon a career in journalism.

So with the door to resuming her marriage now firmly closed, she resolved to cultivate some true self-sufficiency and independence. The plan didn't quite work as she'd hoped. With some level of warped logic, she'd embarked upon an affair with a work colleague called Henry. Knowing he's taken I can't have any expectations, she reasoned, therefore I can't be disappointed. What started off as a heady and
~~~

romantic secret liaison soon came to a crashing halt, when Henry left his wife for her. But the wife was not to be so easily defeated, and mustered the entire emotional forces of her family and friends to pressure him to return, which he did. Then followed three miserable years in which she still saw Henry occasionally, constantly hoping against hope that things might magically work out for them. Now that she was in her late twenties and the biological clock was ticking, she even made the proposition that Henry could father a child for her; she could be a single mother and no one need know. Needless to say, Henry declined the offer, horrified.

So time once more to get a grip. Time to take charge and "be her own person", as psychology books loved to describe it, in their inimitable jargon. No more of this falling headlong in lust with Mr Wrong, hoping he might be Mr Right.

Things seemed to be going well; she was studying horticulture at night school, holding down a rewarding job and having a rich social life, enjoying time with close friends of the female persuasion — the sort who wouldn't break your heart and have you blubbering into your pillow at night.

How did things get so easily derailed? She remembered the night well.

On one of her rare nights at home, she'd been desperate for a cup of coffee only to find the milk had soured in the fridge. The local 7-11 was only a quick walk away, so she decided to pop in there, perhaps to also grab a naughty snack of something forbidden, like a chocolate bar.

To her annoyance, most of the milk she normally used had sold out, but high on the top shelf one lonely carton seemed to be lurking — just out of reach for a short person such as her.

Standing on tippy-toes, hands reaching in vain, she suddenly became aware, with a start, of a figure standing very close to her.

"May I?" asked a warm inviting voice.

She looked up to see a pair of dark brown eyes looking intently at her. (Uh-oh, she'd always been a sucker for voices and eyes.)

"Oh, thanks," she quickly responded, unexpectedly flustered.

The man looked as if he might want to engage in further conversation, but Sarah hastily beat a retreat to the cash register, paid and headed home, where she pondered over the cup of coffee as to why she'd been reluctant to speak with him. After all, he didn't look like the serial killer type. Ah well, a missed opportunity maybe, but she was now so fiercely attached to her hard-won self-sufficiency, just the thought of some random male interrupting it was disturbing. Well, maybe also a little tantalising.

A few days later, she found herself sitting at an Acland Street café, grappling with the cryptic crossword and feeling inexplicably disconsolate. It was one of those lovely days she always thought of as a "Greek day" – not too hot, not too cold, blue sky, slight breeze, and people strolling past, obviously relishing life. It was times like this she felt a twinge of loneliness – how nice it would be to share this halcyon day with a special someone.

Among the passersby, her glance alighted upon a familiar face. A man was planting a kiss on the cheek of a much younger pretty woman and giving her a farewell wave. He turned and headed straight for Sarah's table, pulled out a chair, handed her a business card, and then belatedly asked "May I?"

She suddenly realised where she'd seen him before. "Ah, the

man from the 7-11. Is 'May I' your signature line, and what on earth is this – your business card?" She sounded more confrontational than she had intended, but he just laughed warmly.

"Robert Francis, at your service. You looked so forlorn here, I thought I'd join you. You'd make an excellent photographic subject, sitting here with the sun behind your hair like a halo." His hands rose in a photographic framing gesture, at the same time as Sarah looked at the card he'd given her. Yes, the information on the card tallied with his introduction. He was a professional photographer.

He was fixing her with those eyes again, as he laughed and said, "Ah, true beauty captured and immortalised through the lens."

Both annoyed and charmed, Sarah retorted, "Well, I don't think you'll get far with pick-up lines that that!"

Almost as soon as he'd sat down, Robert was standing up again. "Tell you what, I've got to go but you've got my card so give me a ring and we'll exchange some more meaningful lines … if you'd like."

He departed, blowing her a kiss and leaving her decidedly rattled.

<div style="text-align:center">~~~</div>

She never managed to understand what perverse devil inside her caused her to phone Robert Francis. But there it was, and now she found herself ensconced in a delightfully intimate Italian restaurant, a half-consumed bottle of wine between them, conversation flowing easily and sparks definitely flying. A single iris lay on the table; Robert had presented it to her at the start of the evening, before pulling out her chair to help her sit. The man was a constant surprise.

"How did you know I love irises?" queried Sarah.

"Oh, a lucky guess. And anyway, I love them too. Flowers make such interesting photographic subjects. I'm always on the hunt for new subjects."

"So do you think good photographers are born or made?" asked Sarah.

Robert drained his coffee, pushed the cup away and took a last sip of wine. He leant across the table and looked Sarah intensely in the eye.

"You know how I'll answer that – I've got this great scenic shoot coming up along the Great Ocean Road. You should come along. I could teach you a lot about photography there. It's the most spectacular backdrop."

And so it began, an intensely passionate love affair that coasted along, seemingly trouble-free for about a year. But as Sarah grew more and more attached to the idea that Robert might be "the one", he grew increasingly distant. More and more nights he was inexplicably unavailable, citing a photographic shoot at his studio as the reason she couldn't reach him on the phone.

Negatives left lying around his apartment were testament to the many photo shoots featuring gorgeous young women who apparently all were in need of an urgent modelling portfolio.

"Sarah, I really am over your jealousy," Robert would say when she queried exactly who was who in these shots. "You're making me feel claustrophobic. In fact, I think we could do with a little time apart, just to think things over."

She couldn't believe what she was hearing. After the past year of wonderful times, great sex, vows of love – where was this coming from?

She remembered the weeks (or was it only days?) of howling like a wounded beast, not sleeping, drinking herself into oblivion, trying in vain to raise him on the phone until at last, she was seemingly resigned to the whole thing being over.

But then, one evening, there he was on her doorstep, a bunch of irises in hand, a crestfallen look on his face. Ah, he had a gift with words, with endless plausible excuses.

"Can you ever forgive me? I was just so overtired from all the work, and a bit scared that things had gone too far too fast. You know what a shitty marriage I had, and the thought of another failure like that sometimes freaks me out."

His hand went out to smooth her cheek, his arms clasped her tight and she melted again into his arms, and into the ongoing weeks and months of torment. Some days things were idyllic, Robert seemingly besotted with her; other times he was cold, aloof and almost contemptuous of her needy love for him.

Like an epiphany, one day Sarah realised she could not go on and on like this, riding the rollercoaster of rejection, reconciliation and self-loathing. Out in the garden, viciously wielding secateurs, she muttered viciously out loud to herself.

"What the fuck! How much more shit am I willing to put up with from you, you fucking bastard? I'm worth more than that!"

Immediately upon arriving at work the following Monday, she went to HR and got the form to apply for a year's leave without pay. It seemed the only way. Make a clean break, head off for Europe via Greece, with the intention of staying away a full year.

Her friends were eager to throw a going-away party, and of course, by that time Robert had decided he would be bereft without Sarah, and his full emotions were on display. The night before the going-away party, he almost threw himself at Sarah's feet, sobbing loudly.

"I'm losing the best thing I ever had! Please forgive me. I know you're going to go, but perhaps I could come over and meet you somewhere along the way."

The party with her friends was a grand success, except maybe for Robert's unexpected presence, and during which he sat forlornly, eyes red-rimmed, reproachful. Having him there was perhaps a mistake, but she'd made no commitments about allowing him to visit her overseas, and she felt little could dampen her enthusiasm for her forthcoming adventure.

~~~

Once again the letters and postcards from her trip told their sorry tale. Cards she'd sent to her parents which they had kept were now back with her, telling the superficial story of where she went, what she saw, and what a great time she was having. The letters from Robert told a different tale. He wrote to say he'd thought things over and was actually prepared to have another child with her (he already had a teenage son). So, life was going to finally work out, she thought.

His meeting her at Athens airport was like a scene from a cheesy rom-com, as he leapt the immigration barrier and clasped her in his arms. Together they travelled for several blissful weeks throughout Europe, but then he declared he needed to return to Australia for his work. She was determined to stay on, with the assumption they would live together upon her much later return.

Missing him proved too much for Sarah, so after only four months away, she cut her year-long travels short and headed home. She had no choice but to move in with Robert, as she
~~~

had rented her own home out for the entire year.

She should have recognised the alarm bells early on, when, one evening, he looked at her earnestly and said, "Please don't get pregnant just yet. There's a few too many complications with work to handle another big change in life."

Living with him soon became a nightmare. More and more nights he was out working on his photography, supposedly, and more and more negatives of glamorous, scantily clad models seemed to be lying around on the benchtops of his work space.

Several months later, he announced one night, "This is just not working for me." Tensions and tears in the household were at an all-time high. "You'll need to find somewhere else to live."

Fortunately, Sophie had come to her rescue and Sarah was able to spend time there until her house was finally free again. But, like the true idiotic romantic she was, every time Robert turned up full of professed regrets, she fell into his arms again – until the fateful day he announced he was marrying his first ever girlfriend, the one he'd loved even before he married his ex-wife.

That was the end of that, and Sarah felt a level of deep relief that it was over, even though she hadn't been the one able to end it.

Again, mustering that sense of self-sufficiency, she flew into action, joining a singles club, even becoming a committee member, organising functions and finally regaining a sense of fun in her life.

One of the women she befriended there, Genia, was a single mother who spoke endlessly about her young son Viktor but never alluded to the child's father.

Sarah finally plucked up the courage to ask, "Genia, just who is this mysterious father of your boy?"

"His name was Robert," Genia replied.

"Any surname?"

And when Genia spoke the name, Sarah was aghast. The two women fell into a complex conversation working on dates and times. How could this possibly be?

"I was at a party," Genia told Sarah. "I met this gorgeous guy who looked at me and told me I looked like a French model and he needed to photograph me. He said he'd just split up with his girlfriend, and was feeling a bit down. We sort of clicked and it was full-on from night one."

The date of that party was in the second week after Sarah had left for Europe, the time when Robert was professing undying love for her over long-distance telephone calls. Good God, he'd even said when he came to meet her that he would bring his grandmother's wedding ring with him!

So, while Sarah was waiting for her Prince not-so-charming, he was having a passionate affair with Genia, up until the day she told him she was pregnant.

"You can't do that!" he'd expostulated. "That's genetic robbery!"

After further arguing and remonstrating, he'd added, "Besides, my girlfriend's coming back from overseas, and we'll be getting back together, so I suggest you get an abortion."

Which of course Genia had not done, opting to bring up the child alone, and never receiving a bean from Robert, who denied the existence of the small boy.

If Sarah had felt any lingering affection or nostalgia for Robert, it evaporated with the sad and sorry tale of his duplicity, and what he had done to Genia. (A small postscript was that, ten or so years later, Genia decided to file for a paternity suit. The court-enforced DNA test proved Robert to be the father, and she decided to sue him for child support. Sarah was co-opted to be a possible witness, and when Robert saw Sarah sitting on a bench outside the courtroom, his face blanched whiter than snow. Ah, sweet revenge, Sarah had thought.)

~~~

She picked out each letter which had Robert's distinctive handwriting upon it, and began to tear each one into as many pieces as she could, then tossed them into the fireplace where they would be suitable kindling for the forthcoming winter fire.
~~~

Chapter 28
Are we still right together?

Sitting by the winter fire was small consolation for yet another lockdown being in full swing, implemented by an increasingly desperate and authoritarian government.

Sarah supposed that one positive was that she could spend the entire day not even bothering to change out of her nightgown – what a slob I've become, she thought. Thank God David is not here to see me. But would he have even cared? That old adage *familiarity breeds contempt* was alive and well in so many long-term marriages. Did it apply to her and David, she pondered?

Despite having kept every card they'd ever sent to each other, Sarah wondered if that were mere wishful thinking: a sad attempt to demonstrate to herself that the marriage really had been a love match, that the love was alive and well, and that she hadn't wasted nearly three decades on yet another Mr Wrong.

It wasn't that she didn't love him anymore, she thought; more the sort of thing that happened in a long-term relationship – the cooling of lust, the moments of boredom with one's partner, the inability to truly listen to the other person. Yes, maybe that was one of the biggest things that bugged her about David. When she spoke, it was as if he automatically turned off, sometimes making a grunt in response, other times not even responding at all.

"Did you hear that I spoke to you!?" she would demand, with a mixture of hurt and anger.

A vision came to her of how he would respond to certain

other women, even other men, when they talked. He was capable of sitting in rapt attention, as if every word that dropped from their lips was a gem, even when Sarah found it unutterably boring.

To make matters worse, despite being now semi-retired, he seemed even more obsessed with his work and his creative pursuits than ever before. Not to mention his latest burgeoning obsession with golf. Sometimes as much as three times a week, he spent entire afternoons on the course, and when he wasn't playing, he tried to catch every possible broadcast of championship matches on the cable television.

How this had all fitted in with his work was a mystery to her; often when she had wanted to spend an afternoon doing something together, he had made work the excuse, but it never seemed to interfere with his sporting activities.

She couldn't deny it, of late they'd been drifting apart, arguing more often, making love less frequently and doing more things separately. A part of her missed the fun times they'd had together. She started to occasionally wonder if she'd made yet another bad decision regarding a man.

Having freelance clients still enabled him to use work as an excuse. Now look where it had got him! Stuck overseas in the middle of a pandemic. She wondered how he was taking it. Perhaps relieved and happy to be away from her? Which all led her to wonder if perhaps she wasn't just a convenience to him. A pleasant companion who did most of the cooking and the household chores, but who he took mostly for granted. Perhaps this time apart would lead them both to make some rather radical decisions.

Chapter 29
Harry misbehaves yet again

The letters found after Harry's death were not only between him and Angela. No, there was more to come, as Sarah was to discover reading through the more recent correspondence unearthed from the stash in Harry's cupboards.

Angela's and Harry's marriage was in tatters but not yet officially dissolved. Despite the fact that he was still living with Angela, letters revealed that he had obviously been attending some sort of dating club and had met woman after woman, hopeful of rekindling some of his self-image as a desirable playboy. Or maybe it was kinder to believe he was just lonely. Sarah learned that women had either fallen head over heels in love with him, or had been totally affronted by his forward nature, including unwelcomed groping of their ample bodies.

One letter read:

Dear Harry, You seemed such a nice man when we first met, but I must tell you I did not welcome the way you placed your hands upon my breasts. I really think we should not see each other again.

But then he had met Jennifer, a lonely divorced woman who had just come out of a psychiatric institute. It seemed they'd been having a torrid on and off affair, in which she alternately declared undying love for him, and then berated him for being hard-hearted and unable to make up his mind about her.

Somewhere in the dim recesses of memory, Sarah remembered Angela talking about this sad and sorry situation. Having just finalised her divorce from Richy, and being between apartments, Sarah was living for a brief few weeks with her parents again, waiting to find suitable accommodation. She overheard her mother on the phone to Sheila.

"He needs to get his act together, does Harry. Thinking he can just swan around, while I cook meals, do the ironing and washing, and he agonises over whether to go to this crazy woman or stay with me."

It was Angela's doctor who eventually made the decision for them. Seeing the fragile nature of Angela's mental health, he declared that she should remove herself for a period of time so she could get her strength back. Just where she went Sarah never remembered, but when she returned, probably having undergone some serious counselling, she had strengthened her resolve and told Harry that time was finally up for them.

She had always been terrified of being unable to support herself, and that had probably aided in her delaying the inevitable. But incredibly, Harry came to a momentous decision. Realising that he could always support himself, albeit modestly, with his musical gigs, he decided to sign the marital home over to Angela, giving her the much-needed security she desired.

Tail between his legs, perhaps having found some redemption in such a generous act, he headed off to a small council flat, enough room for one, and breathing space to continue machinating over Jennifer.

Unfortunately for Harry, Jennifer plunged into one of her psychotic episodes and decided to attack him with a vegetable knife, finally making the decision for him that he would be better off without her. Back to the drawing board and the singles clubs.

Chapter 30
Angela takes an extreme step

No matter how difficult a time a person has with a partner, after so many years together there is a void and a gap. Perhaps Angela had seen herself, in some warped way, as Harry's saviour, or even as his minder; a sort of caring parent who kept him from tipping over the edge. Now she no longer had that purpose in her life and, despite the relief of the removal of the endless tension, she felt strangely bereft.

She became very needy, and began to put a guilt trip upon Sarah, constantly berating her daughter for not telephoning often enough.

"Why can't you be like Betty's daughter and ring every day?"

The more Angela pushed, the further Sarah pulled away. After all, she didn't need such closeness with her mother. Her move into journalism had eventually landed her an amazing job, with a team of fun people writing magazines for school kids. Going to work and being paid was really just an excuse for having fun.

She shared an office space with Paul, a jovial, witty man who had met both of Sarah's parents, and who liked to make fun and joke about anything and everything.

"So, how's your old cheese going?" he asked out of the blue one day.

"Oh, I wouldn't know," Sarah replied blithely.

Paul looked unusually concerned. "Well, she has been through a rough patch. She could be feeling depressed. Maybe you should ring her."

Sarah looked taken aback. "She's becoming a real pain these days, always hounding me."

"Oh come on, Sar, she's your mum. Just give her a quick buzz."

"Oh, whatever! Don't know why you care so much."

She picked up the phone and listened to the ringing at the other end. It went on and on. Just as she was about to hang up the ringing stopped and the phone was picked up. But there was no voice at her mother's end.

"Mum! Hello? Are you there? What's happening!?"

She heard a clatter as if the phone were dropped from someone's hand, and a chill ran through her. Instinctively she knew something was amiss.

Thinking laterally, Sarah got her little address book out of her handbag and quickly found the phone number for her mother's next-door neighbour. Again the phone seemed to ring incessantly. Feeling totally alarmed now, she muttered under her breath, "Oh, come on!"

Paul looked on, curious and worried.

"Hello!" A breathless voice answered.

"Oh, thank heavens. Sorry to bother you, Larry, it's your neighbour's daughter, Sarah."

"Sarah, I was just locking up and leaving for work. What's up?"

"I might be crazy but I have this really weird feeling something bad has happened to my mother. Would it be too much trouble to just go there and see if you can roust her up?"

"No problem. Come to think of it, she has looked rather unwell the last few times I've seen her. I'll ring you back as soon as I speak to her. Give me your work number."

The wait seemed interminable until, with pounding heart, Sarah snatched up the phone. Her face paled as she listened. Hanging up, she turned to Paul.

"You were right. The neighbour said after he rang the doorbell for a few minutes, he was about to give up, but then the door was answered by a naked woman all covered in blood, seeming drunk or drugged. He rang the ambulance and sent her to the nearest hospital."

~~~

Angela looked pale and almost childlike lying there in the hospital bed, both wrists heavily bandaged.

The nurse had assured Sarah that her mother would be okay; it seemed she had used the razor blade horizontally, which, while causing a lot of blood loss, would not be enough to kill her. She also had a huge amount of whisky and many sleeping pills in her system, but a stomach pump had taken care of that.

The guilt that washed over Sarah was almost unbearable. Gently she took her mother's limp hand.

"I love you, Mum. What on earth did you do this for?"

Angela's eyelids fluttered open and a smile spread across her face.

"Oh, nurse. You are so lovely! You remind me of my daughter." The eyes closed again and Angela fell into a **deep** sleep while Sarah just sat, stunned, looking at her mother and praying it would all be alright in the end.

~~~

It was, in fact, more than alright. After recovering from her suicide attempt, Angela slowly started to piece her life together again. Part of the healing was to travel back to her beloved England, to visit with her brother and see some of the old haunts.

She wrote many a postcard to Sarah. Somehow, the adventure seemed to be making her stronger as she realised she could do things that even the thought of had once sent her into a fit of anxiety. Even more surprising was her assertion that England had changed beyond recognition and that she realised now, after so many years, she was an Aussie.

Upon her return, she launched into studies at the University of the Third Age, where she enrolled in an art class and a literature class. She also ran a small theatre improvisation class. There she met a man, Morrell, a soft-spoken widower who finally showed her that a man could not only be faithful, but could make her happy.

The happiness was not to last for too long. Fate had other things in store for Angela.

After all the years of using her voice in the theatre, she had suffered often from continuous sore throats. Her local GP back in the 1970s had been a typically patriarchal doctor who thought he was some species of God. No one ever even called him by his name; he was just "Doctor", as if that title bestowed all manner of wisdom upon him.

Angela visited him regularly, desperate to know how to cure her sore throat.

With a look of contempt on his face, the doctor had declared, "You are acting like a hysterical menopausal woman. Go home and have a good inhalation over a bowl of Vicks Vaporub."

Sarah remembered the many nights of her mother leaning over a steaming bowl, towel over her head, inhaling deeply, hoping there could be some relief.

Then, all those years later, now married to Morrell, she had finished with theatre but still suffered terrible throat problems. She finally found a doctor prepared to spend the time to examine more thoroughly what was going on. A gastroscope revealed the worst news – advanced throat cancer which would necessitate the removal of her larynx. That beautiful speaking voice would no longer enchant the world – she would be rendered mute and have to use one of those ghastly "Dalek machines" to enable her to speak.

Angela battled on for two more years before finally succumbing to her cancer.

So many of the cards Sarah had kept had been sent to Angela from friends, praising her bravery, along with cards sent to Sarah and to Morrell, expressing their condolences, and describing just what a wonderful woman Angela had been.

Happiness for Angela at last

Chapter 31

Sarah revisits more men from the past

How much more trawling through her past failed love affairs Sarah could tolerate, she didn't know.

What further mortifying evidence would be found in these countless folders of scribblings? In the first one she opened there were seemingly endless and agonised outpourings she had committed to paper over the various men who had caused her grief. Then there were the outpourings from some of the men, some handwritten, some typed, most containing words expressing just how much Sarah had meant to them, even if their actions hadn't matched their words. Some of it was amusing, some sad and some downright disturbing. The pattern of unavailable men she'd wasted her time on was what disturbed her most.

A bulging folder of letters from the lengthy Henry affair revealed what a fabulous writer he was, and how he had always managed to imbue her with a glimmer of hope that somehow fate would intervene and allow them to be together. He couldn't admit that his fate was actually in his own hands – he just couldn't swim against the tide of the pressures of kids and family, and make the decision to leave his wife. How ironic that it was meeting Robert that had finally helped her make the break from Henry.

Then there were the amusing and witty love poems from Jeremy, another work colleague who had come to live in the city from a rural life where he'd run the local newspaper. Yes, he and his wife were over and done with, he swore it, but he did have to make the occasional visit back to his home town to check in on the children. How naïve Sarah had been to believe any of his persuasive stories. After a year of what was in fact a lot of fun together, Jeremy declared he was returning to his wife because she was unwell.

It was shocking to Sarah, but the real shock came over their farewell dinner, before Jeremy left both Sarah and Melbourne forever. After a few too many drinks, he garrulously revealed that not only was the wife stashed away in the country town, but also a next-door neighbour with whom he'd been having an affair for ten years!

And here were Valentine's cards from sweet Phillipe, a French man she'd met at a single's club. They had danced the night away, he had told her he was separated from his wife, but that they still lived in the same house but in separate rooms. The instant attraction and whirlwind romance saw Phillipe pluck up the courage to move out from his wife and take up residence with Sarah. Maybe finally, she had thought, this could be the one.

But spurned wives have a way of putting spokes in wheels, and Phillipe's wife grew angry and jealous. She would drive her car in the early hours of the morning, park outside Sarah's house and wait until Phillipe left for work. Then she would cut him off, jump out of her car, and swear to him she would kill herself if he did not come home. Of course, he had crumbled under the pressure and returned home.

~~~

Hours passed quickly as Sarah wallowed in her past, until she finally felt fed up with it all and somewhat ashamed of her past weaknesses. Steeling herself, she began to screw up the pages one by one, and tossed them into the fire.

A vision of David popped into her head, and she started
~~~

to reflect on the things that had drawn her to him. One characteristic stood out loud and clear. Basically, Sarah had realised early on that he was a truly decent bloke, someone who was honest and kind, someone who, she hoped, would never cheat on her the way so many of the men in her past had, the way Harry had cheated on Angela. Sure, David wasn't one for flowery speeches and tokens of affection, but he was loyal and true, and always stood up for her and was supportive when she had faced any sort of crisis. It was no wonder how reliable David had seemed after this motley assortment of men.

Sarah fell to musing on just what kept people together. Some people felt they had to have 90 per cent to stay in a relationship. Others settled for just over the halfway mark. Others really sold out, the way Angela had stuck it out with Harry, long after the marriage had passed its use-by date. Sarah just wasn't quite sure what percentage she now had with David.

Chapter 32
When Harry met Helen

While Angela's final years had been ultimately happy, despite her ghastly illness, Harry had also stumbled upon a measure of peace and contentment.

He still did the occasional evening gig with his violin, but more often he went out to old folks homes during the day, playing for the residents and bringing them joy, as his music ignited memories of their past. He was so appreciated that the local council had given him an award in acknowledgment.

Somewhere along the way, he'd met a delightful woman, Helen, also of English background, a gently-spoken widow who lived in a little flat, and loved to cook for Harry, go to movies with him, or just stay home watching TV together.

"Isn't she lovely, my Helen? But you know your old Papa is a bit of a cradle snatcher. She's at least nine years younger than I am, you know!"

Sarah hadn't remembered seeing her father so happy as those times he was together with his new love. She remembered having entertained the pair for dinner, and being invited in return to a meal with Helen and Harry. All so civilised, amiable and warm; such a contrast to the life he'd shared with Angela.

Sarah had to chuckle as she remembered that Helen actually had the last laugh, even though Harry had still been up to his old deceptive tricks up until the end.

At Harry's funeral, Sarah had given a eulogy and placed a photograph on the coffin, with the years of his birth and death revealing him to have died at the age of seventy-nine.

As she chatted afterwards over a cup of tea with Helen, the older woman said to Sarah, "Oh, I never knew his real age. He was such a varmint, wasn't he! He told me he was seventy, you know. And he thought he was the cradle snatcher." She paused for effect. "But I'll be eighty-three next birthday, you know!"

Amidst her sadness for Harry's death, Sarah couldn't help but laugh out loud.

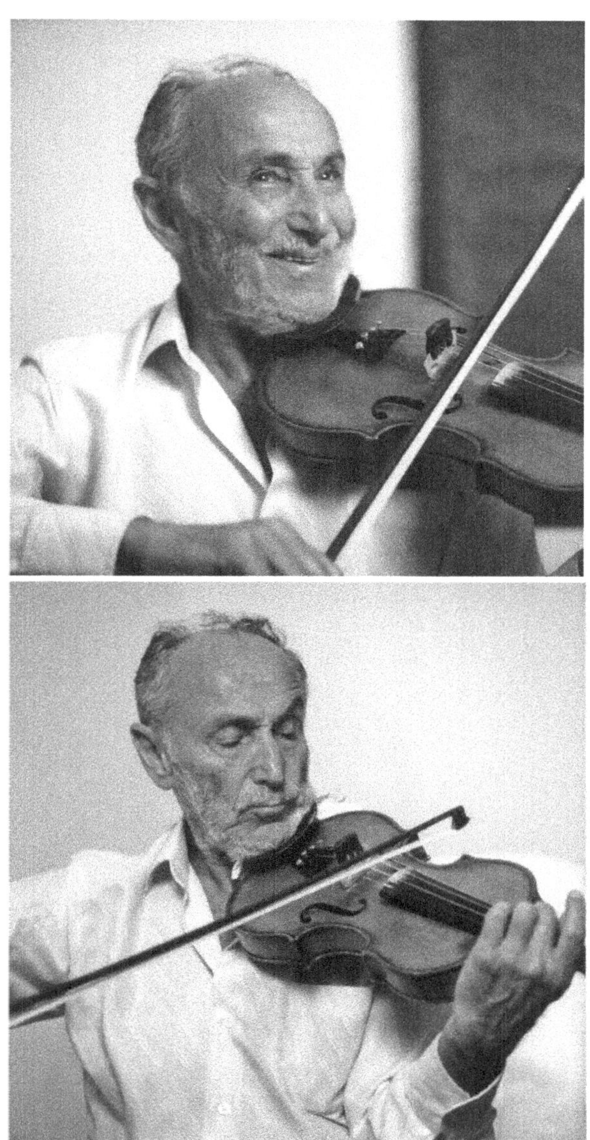

Harry, at age 73, doing what he did best

Chapter 33
A wake-up call

At three in the morning Sarah's mobile phone rang. Normally she put it on silent at night, but with David still stuck overseas she thought better of it.

He rang her every week or so, but there was not a lot to say as they were both stuck for the time being in their respective countries. Even when lockdowns lifted slightly, airlines were in chaos, flights were limited and expensive, and until now he had been unable to get a flight out. The only one he'd managed to book had been cancelled at the last minute.

Groggy from sleep, she picked up the phone.

An unfamiliar voice with a British accent cut into the early morning hours. After ascertaining her identity, the caller didn't waste time on niceties.

"It's the Hammersmith Hospital here. Your husband David has been in an accident. He's in intensive care. If there is any possibility of getting a flight over, I suggest you do it."

Her heart lurched and she was instantly wide awake. Her first thought was how to get out of the country.

Of course there were a few flights, but getting one was the challenge and it would cost a fortune. But money was not the issue here. Getting to be with her husband was all that mattered.

~~~

Less than forty-eight hours later, she was cruising at 30,000 feet, halfway between Melbourne and London. Normally she relaxed on a flight, looked forward to meals and films, but
~~~

this time, sitting there under her mask and feeling agitated, all she could think about was David. The doctor she'd spoken to had not been overly optimistic. What condition would she find him in, would he even be alive, how would she cope without him?

That last question hit a nerve. Despite all the misgivings of late, all the gripes, grizzles and arguments, she knew deep down he was her rock, her anchor in life, her partner in good times and bad, connected by almost thirty years of sharing together, being a witness to each other's lives, and for her he was definitely the most important person in her life.

~~~

She sat by David's bedside, holding his hand and looking sorrowfully at his poor bruised face. She could only wonder what the internal damage looked like.

David's supervising doctor set her mind at ease. It seemed when the phone call was made, no conclusive scan or x-ray results were yet available; staff at the hospital had merely thought it best to get "the wife" over there, just in case. According to the doctor, the past couple of days had seen a dramatic improvement in his condition, and scans had revealed no brain damage and no life-threatening organ injuries, despite their initial concern.

~~~

By the time David was discharged from hospital, there were many more available international flights and there hadn't been a lockdown for a couple of months. Well, if there were any more to come, they would at least share them under the one roof.

Several weeks later, Sarah and David sat by the open fire, a glass of wine in hand. He glanced up at a photo of Angela and Harry that Sarah had relocated from another room to take pride of place on the fireplace mantelshelf. Angela looked glamorous in a 1950s frock, pearl earrings and a white shawl. Although she smiled, there was a hint of sadness and wistful longing in her eyes. Harry, dapper in suit and bow tie, looked at the camera full-on, a hint of a smile, perhaps proud to be with this beautiful woman, perhaps chastened to know he might only bring her grief. They appeared to be dining together at a fancy restaurant.

"It's such a lovely photo," remarked Sarah, following David's gaze. "I wish they had found happiness together."

He reached across, uncharacteristically, and took Sarah's hand, gently stroking her fingers.

"I had some awful nightmares in the hospital before you arrived, you know," he ventured. As she looked questioningly at him, he continued: "I'd got home from golf to find the house was empty. I knew instinctively you'd run off with another man. I sat and sobbed then smashed up my computer with a golf club."

"Hmm," was all she had to say, suppressing a laugh.

"It was like an epiphany. I realised I'd been spending too much time pursuing my own stuff and really all I wanted was to pull back from it all, just spend time with you, maybe travel a bit in Oz when this wretched virus passes."

After a pause he added, "I actually thought I might have died without telling you that I couldn't bear to lose you, Sarah. You really are the world to me."

Abruptly changing the tone, he asked, "What on earth are those piles of papers you've got there?"

"Just the leftovers of past people who caused a lot of grief in my life," she responded, grabbing a few more pages,

The romanticism and glamour belied the truth.

crumpling them, and tossing them into the fire.

"You're not going to throw out any of those letters you told me about, you know, the ones from your parents, I hope?" he queried.

"Oh God no – those lives are hard-wired into my being. I feel I understand them so much better now. It's all been a bit of a revelation."

She sat thoughtfully for a few minutes.

"Perhaps I'll write them into some sort of a memoir one day," she said, surprised and pleased at her own suggestion.

"What about all these other bits of memorabilia?" he asked,

gesturing at the ever-diminishing pile of papers.

"Oh, I guess they've played their roles and led me to where I am now. Probably wouldn't have appreciated the good things about you if I hadn't had all those roller-coaster-ride times!"

"Hell, I hope you're not going to include all the gory details of your love affairs!"

"Well, no, but no one will know what's really true, and what's been embellished. That's the fun of being a writer – record your history, imagine your future and embroider the edges where you see fit."

THE END